Lambda Calculi

Graduate Texts in Computer Science

Editors

D. M. Gabbay, C. L. Hankin, and T. S. E. Maibaum

GRADUATE TEXTS IN COMPUTER SCIENCE

Lambda Calculi

A guide for computer scientists

CHRIS HANKIN

Department of Computing,
Imperial College of Science, Technology, and Medicine,
London

CLARENDON PRESS · OXFORD
1994

Oxford University Press, Walton Street, Oxford OX2 6DP

Oxford New York
Athens Auckland Bangkok Bombay
Calcutta CapeTown DaresSalaam Delhi
Florence HongKong Istanbul Karachi
KualaLumpur Madras Madrid Melbourne
MexicoCity Nairobi Paris Singapore
Taipei Tokyo Toronto

and associated companies in
Berlin Ibadan

Oxford is a trade mark of Oxford University Press

Published in the United States by
Oxford University Press Inc., New York

A catalogue record for this book is available from the British Library

Library of Congress Cataloging in Publication Data
(Data available)

ISBN 0 19 853841 3 (hbk)
ISBN 0 19 853840 5 (pbk)

Typeset by the author

Printed in Great Britain by
Bookcraft (Bath) Ltd
Midsomer Norton, Avon

Preface

The λ-calculus, alongside Turing machines and Recursive Function Theory, is of foundational importance to the theory of computation. While the λ-calculus and Recursive Function Theory promote a programming-based view of computation, the Turing machine approach is machine-based. Surprisingly, it is the machine-based approach which has been most popular in undergraduate computability courses. One side effect of the current popularity of functional programming in the undergraduate curriculum is that most undergraduate computer scientists now receive some introduction to the λ-calculus as well. However, few undergraduate students see more than the syntax, some consideration of reduction strategies and statements of the key Church–Rosser and Standardisation Theorems.

In contrast, anyone embarking on a research career in theoretical computer science is soon faced with a bewildering variety of formal calculi. Many concepts which appear in their simplest form in the λ-calculus recur again and again. There is thus a pedagogical gap to be filled between the superficial undergraduate treatment of this material and the more detailed understanding required as a basis for research. Despite this, a new book on the type-free λ-calculus still requires some justification, since:

- There is already an encyclopaedic book on the topic (Barendregt), which has become the standard reference text, and there is an excellent textbook (Hindley and Seldin).

- In both the logic and the computer science communities, the main research interest is now in typed calculi.

Regarding the first point, in contrast to either of the two books mentioned above, this book was written by a computer scientist and is specifically targetted at a computer science audience. I strongly believe that there is a distinct cultural difference between computer science students and their mathematically trained counterparts. The former have sound computational intuitions but are generally unfamiliar and uncomfortable with formalism. While the two books mentioned were written with a mathematically mature audience in mind, I have attempted to provide more computing-oriented motivation. Furthermore, my selection of material for inclusion in this book has been informed by this desire to communicate to computer scientists. The material on needed reductions, reduction machines, abstract interpretation, Hindley–Milner polymorphism, lazy calculi and concurrent calculi is all distinctive compared to the earlier books. Indeed, given that the two books mentioned above are, respectively, 10 and 8 years old, much of this new material has been developed since they were published.

Why not study typed calculi? The pure λ-calculus (type-free $\lambda K\beta$-calculus) is probably the simplest of the family of λ-calculi. While the emphasis has recently shifted to typed calculi, many of the basic issues remain the same. In other areas, such as concurrency, the majority of the calculi proposed and studied are still type-free. The concepts that we deal with in the following pages recur in many different areas of computing: programming languages, semantics, concurrency and even databases! Every graduate computer scientist should have some familiarity with this material.

In common with any other formal system, there are two major aspects of the λ-calculus; its *proof theory* and its *model theory*. I have decided to concentrate on the proof theory. This is a rich theory which has many connections to practical computing; some of which we investigate in the sequel. The model theory of the λ-calculus, which is abstractly discussed in Chapter 5, takes us into the realms of domain theory and is properly treated in a course on denotational semantics or domain theory. There are already a number of excellent textbooks on this material.

I first taught some of this material in 1983, during a six hour seminar to first year graduate students. The course later grew to ten hours and then, finally, to a twenty hour lecture course. In its current form it is taught to fourth year undergraduate students and students studying on a one year Masters course.

My intention is that there should be enough material in this book to allow the instructor to tailor an appropriate course but not too much material so that prospective students become intimidated. I have never taught all of the material to a single cohort of students. I estimate that to do so would require about thirty hours of lecture time. The shorter courses that I have taught concentrated on the first three chapters. The basic course (core material) that I now teach covers most of the first six chapters, the simply typed λ-calculus (the first section of Chapter 7) and some of Chapter 8. The material in Chapters 8 and 9 is more research-oriented; I cover as much of this as possible.

In writing this book, I have assumed a minimal amount of background knowledge. Students who have attended a standard Computer Science Course on discrete mathematics covering logic and set theory should be well-prepared for the technical material. It would be an advantage if the reader has also had some exposure to functional programming.

As with any project which has taken so long to reach fruition, many people have influenced its development. I extend my heartfelt thanks to them all. The main acknowledgement should go to the students who have attended (and endured!) my lectures over the last ten years; I, at least, enjoyed my lectures and learnt something new every time! The last two years have been the most critical; during that time, David Clark, Roy Crole, Lindsay Errington, Anthony McIsaac and Ian Mackie all provided valuable input. Geoffrey Burn lectured the course during the 1989/90 academic session and provided the needed stimulus for another evolutionary step. Thomas Jensen kindly read through an earlier draft and gave me some valuable comments and much-needed Latex advice. The Theory and Formal Methods section in the Department of Computing has provided a fertile and supportive environment for me for the last ten years; Samson Abramsky, Dov Gabbay and Tom Maibaum have been good friends and sources of inspiration during that time. Daniel Le Métayer and another, anonymous, reviewer kindly commented on the penultimate version of the manuscript; I thank them for their careful reading – of course, the errors that remain are all mine! Last but not least, I should acknowledge the support of my long-suffering family: Alison Holtorp, my wife, and Emily and David.

Chris Hankin

Imperial College, London
May 1994

Contents

1

Introduction

Overview

We informally introduce the λ-calculus and introduce the reader to a number of concepts and techniques which will recur throughout the book. We start with a discussion of the rôle of functional abstraction in Computer Science; this leads naturally to an informal presentation of the λ-calculus. The λ-calculus is an example of a formal system; we include a brief introduction to formal systems. Our treatment of the material in this book is quite rigorous; we include proofs of most of the main results and where we do not, the reader is encouraged to provide them (in the exercises). The majority of proofs are inductive; we will introduce the different forms of inductive argument as required but we conclude this chapter with a revision of mathematical induction.

1.1 Functions

One of the universal notions of programming languages is functional abstraction. The SUBROUTINEs and FUNCTIONs of FORTRAN, the PROCEDUREs of Pascal and the functions defined and used in functional programming languages are all instances of this general notion. The inspiration for this form of abstraction mechanism comes from Mathematical Logic; notably Church's λ(lambda)-calculi and Schönfinkel's and Curry's Combinatory Logic. A proper study of these foundations leads to a better understanding of some of the fundamental issues in Computer Science. Areas in which they have had a major influence include:

Programming Language Design: We have already suggested the link with the notion of functional abstraction in programming languages. In addition, many of the typing notions found in modern programming languages have been inspired by the typing mechanisms found in these formal calculi. A notable example of this, to which we shall return, is the style of *polymorphism* which is employed in modern functional programming languages.

Programming Language Semantics: One of the predominant schools of thought on this topic is *denotational semantics*. In this approach a typed λ-calculus is used as the meta-language; the meaning of a program is expressed by mapping it into a corresponding λ-calculus object. Understanding what such objects are requires that we should have a *model* of the calculus; the construction of such models has been the motivation for the subject of *domain theory*.

Computability: A classical use of the λ-calculus was in the study of computability; the study of the theoretical limitations of formal systems for describing computations. Indeed the first result in computability was a result concerning the relationship between the λ-calculus and Kleene's Recursive Functions. The (un-)decidability results familiar from automata theory have their analogues in the theory of the λ-calculus.

As readers study this book, they may well be able to identify other areas in which the formal systems that we are discussing have had an influence.

Classically, in set theory, a function is represented by its *graph*. The graph of a function defines a function by its input/output behaviour; for example, a unary function is represented by a set of pairs where the first component of each pair specifies the argument and the second component specifies the corresponding result. From this perspective, the function on pairs of natural numbers which adds its two arguments is represented as:

$$\{((0,0),0),((0,1),1),\ldots,((1,0),1),((1,1),2),\ldots\}$$

or:

$$\{((m,n),p) \mid m,n \in Num, p = n + m\}$$

Two functions are equal if they have the same graph; later this notion of equality will be referred to as *extensional* equality.

From the point of view of Computer Science, this representation is not very useful. We are usually as interested in *how* a function computes its answer as in *what* it computes. For example, all sorting functions have the same graph and are thus (extensionally) equal but a large part of the Computer Science literature has been devoted to the definition and analysis of different sorting algorithms, so we are clearly missing something. The casual use of the word "algorithm" in the last sentence is the key; we should represent a function by a rule, which describes how the result is calculated, rather than its graph. In this scheme, two functions are equal if they are both defined by the same (or equivalent) rules; this form of equality is called *intensional* equality. The λ-calculus[1] provides a formalism for expressing functions as *rules of correspondence* between arguments and results and will be the main system discussed in this book.

---

[1]There is a wide variety of different λ-calculi. The calculi differ along many axes: syntax, typing, rules of inference,.... When we talk of the λ-calculus we generally mean the pure, type-free $\lambda K\beta$-calculus which is the primary object of study in Barendregt's encyclopaedic book.

The λ-calculus consists of a notation for expressing rules, λ-notation, and a set of axioms and rules which tell us how to compute with terms expressed in the notation. A BNF specification of the λ-notation is:

$$
\begin{array}{lll}
< \lambda\text{-term}> & ::= & <\text{variable}> \mid \\
& & (\lambda <\text{variable}>< \lambda\text{-term}>) \mid \quad\quad \textbf{(abs)} \\
& & (< \lambda\text{-term}>< \lambda\text{-term}>) \quad\quad\quad\quad \textbf{(app)} \\
<\text{variable}> & ::= & x \mid y \mid z \dots
\end{array}
$$

Some λ-terms[2] are:

$$x \quad (xz) \quad ((xz)(yz)) \quad (\lambda x(\lambda y(\lambda z((xz)(yz)))))$$

The intuition is that terms matching **(abs)** correspond to function definitions, where the variable after the λ specifies the name of the formal parameter, and terms matching **(app)** correspond to function applications. Thus a first attempt at defining the addition function might be:

$$(\lambda x(\lambda y((+x)y)))$$

but beware! — the symbol + has no intrinsic meaning, according to our syntax it must be just another variable. In Chapter 3 we show how new computation rules (called δ-rules) can be added to the calculus to give the expected meaning to +. Alternatively, the operator can be defined in the pure calculus; this is discussed in Chapter 6, where a more accurate, but less perspicuous, encoding is presented.

A major limitation of the notation seems to be that we can only define unary functions; we can only introduce one formal argument at a time. The fact that this is not a real restriction was first observed by Schönfinkel. Given some binary function denoted by an expression in formal arguments x and y, say $f(x,y)$, then we define:

$$a \equiv (\lambda y(\lambda x(f(x,y))))$$

then a is equivalent to the original function but takes its arguments one at a time[3] .

1.2 Formal Systems

The λ-calculus is an example of a formal system. A formal system is a completely symbolic language built from some alphabet and some rules for manipulating "terms" of the language. Formal systems are commonplace in mathematics. Before embarking on our detailed study of the λ-calculus,

---

[2]If you are confused by all of the parentheses, don't despair! In the next Chapter we will introduce some conventions, which allow us to omit most of them.

[3]A function such as a, which takes its arguments one at a time, is often called a *curried* function (in honour of the logician Haskell B. Curry).

it is instructive to establish some of the terminology and concepts that are common to all formal systems.

The three main aspects of formal systems that we will be concerned with are:

Notation: defining the set of terms (or "well-formed formulae" (wff)).

Theories: giving a set of axioms and rules relating terms.

Models: giving a "mathematical" semantics to the system.

The notation is normally specified in two parts; first the alphabet is presented and then the syntax of terms is presented.

Theories are presented as a set of given theorems, the axioms, and a set of rules for deriving new theorems. We will usually write:

$$T \vdash thm$$

if the theorem *thm* is provable in the theory T; i.e. *thm* is an axiom or derivable from the axioms using the rules and other derived theorems. We will usually be interested in theories of equality between terms; in such a theory, each theorem relates a pair of equal terms. Theories of this form provide a basis for symbol pushing semantics.

The purpose of a model is to give a "meaning" to the terms. An *interpretation* is used to define the value that each term denotes. If all of the theorems are still valid under a particular interpretation, then the interpretation provides a model for the theory. This concept is best illustrated by example: an interpretation of propositional calculus is a mapping from propositions to truth values; it is a model if all valid propositions are true.

Examples of formal systems that the reader might be familiar with include propositional calculus, predicate calculus, CCS,....

1.3   Mathematical Induction

We briefly review mathematical induction which is based on Peano's fifth axiom:

(PA V): if S is a subset of N, $0 \in S$ and $n \in S \Rightarrow succ(n) \in S$ then $S = N$[4]

So when we use mathematical induction to prove some predicate, we require a basis step which shows that 0 satisfies the predicate and then, under the assumption that it is true for some n, we show it is true for $succ(n)$ and then (PA V) states that it is true for all natural numbers. An example of the technique is:

---

[4]N is the set of natural numbers (including zero) and $succ(n)$ is the successor of n.

Example 1.1 $\sum_{i=0..n} i = n(n+1)/2$

Proof

Basis *(n = 0): left hand side = right hand side = 0*

Inductive Hypothesis: *assume* $\sum_{i=0..k} i = k(k+1)/2$ *for some* k

Inductive Step:

$$\sum_{i=0..k+1} i = \sum_{i=0..k} i + (k+1)$$
$$= k(k+1)/2 + (k+1) \text{ by the Inductive Hypothesis (IH)}$$
$$= (k^2 + 3k + 2)/2$$
$$= (k+1)(k+2)/2$$

$\square$

We will often omit the formal statement of the inductive hypothesis from such proofs.

Exercise 1.3.1 *Prove that for any natural number n, there are exactly $n!$ permutations of n objects.*

We will introduce other forms of induction as required throughout the text.

1.4 Summary

We started this chapter by trying to whet the reader's appetite for the study of the λ-calculus and related formalisms. We then presented the two contrasting views of functions: the classical mathematical view in which a function is no more than a graph and the computational view in which a function is a rule of correspondence. We have argued that the latter is a more appropriate view for use in Computer Science.

The ideas and terminology used in this chapter will be used again and again in this book as we study one formal system after another. In the next chapter we will start our study of the λ-calculus and we will progress through combinatory logic, simply typed λ-calculus to the 2nd-order polymorphic λ-calculus and the $\lambda\cap$-calculus.

2

Notation and the Basic Theory

Overview

We now start our study of the λ-calculus. First, we return to the question of notation and present an inductive definition of λ-terms and some auxiliary notions such as *free variables* and *subterms*. Next, we present the theory. Central to the theory is the notion of substitution — the driving force behind function application — we next discuss a number of alternative approaches to defining substitution and consider some of the properties of substitution. The theory is a theory of equality between terms; as indicated in the last chapter, we are trying to capture intensional equality but we also show how the theory can be extended to capture extensional equality. Finally, we consider the consistency and "completeness" of the two theories presented.

2.1 Notation

We will give an inductive definition of λ-terms. This style of definition may be slightly unfamiliar to Computer Scientists so we start by illustrating the approach in the context of the (more familiar) propositional calculus.

The well-formed formulae of propositional calculus are constructed from propositional variables, parentheses and two connectives: unary $\neg$ and binary $\vee$. Of course, this does not define the class of well-formed formulae; however, it does define the *alphabet* which can be used. A wff is a word[1] and we must now define which words are wffs. A Computer Science approach to this problem might be to define a BNF-style syntax for wffs:

$$\begin{aligned}
<\text{wff}> \quad ::= \quad & <\text{variable}> \mid \\
& \neg <\text{wff}> \mid \\
& (<\text{wff}> \vee <\text{wff}>)
\end{aligned}$$

This is what we did for λ-terms in Chapter 1. More usually, the class of wffs is defined *inductively*.

Definition 2.1 *The class, $\mathcal{W}$, of well-formed formulae for the propositional calculus, is the least class such that:*

(1) $p \in \mathcal{W}$ for each propositional variable p

---

[1] A *word* is just a string of characters drawn from the alphabet.

(2) *If A is a formula and $A \in \mathcal{W}$ then $\neg A \in \mathcal{W}$*

(3) *If A and B are formulae and $A, B \in \mathcal{W}$ then $(A \vee B) \in \mathcal{W}$*

By convention, upper case letters will be used to represent arbitrary terms and lower case letters will be used to represent variables. Notice that we take the least class which satisfies the three conditions; any class that contained the wffs and some arbitrary other "terms" would satisfy these conditions, so we take the least (smallest) class to ensure that we don't get the junk!

Some examples of wffs are:

$$a \quad b \quad \neg a \quad (\neg a \vee b)$$

Terms which have the form of the last example, where a and b may be replaced by arbitrary wff, will be written as $a \Rightarrow b$ in the sequel.

λ-terms: The class of λ-terms consists of words constructed from the following alphabet:

$$x, y, z, \ldots \text{ variables}$$
$$\lambda$$
$$(,) \qquad \text{parentheses}$$

We define terms formally as follows:

Definition 2.2 (λ-terms)
The class Λ of λ-terms is the least class satisfying the following:

(1) *$x \in \Lambda$, x a variable*

(2) *if $M \in \Lambda$ then $(\lambda x M) \in \Lambda$*

(3) *if $M, N \in \Lambda$ then $(MN) \in \Lambda$*

Terms constructed by clause 2 are called abstractions; these correspond to functions/procedures in programming languages. The variable following the λ symbol corresponds to the formal parameter of the abstraction and M is the body of the abstraction. Thus:

$$(\lambda xx)$$

should be compared to:

```
(LAMBDA (x) (x))
```

in LISP, or to:

```
FUNCTION id(x:integer):integer;
    BEGIN id := x END;
```

in PASCAL[2]. To avoid the proliferation of parentheses, we will generally use an alternative notation for terms constructed according to clause 2 of the definition:

$$\lambda x.M$$

and moreover, we will elide internal λs and "."s and assume that abstraction associates to the right so that the following terms are equivalent:

$$\lambda x_1 \ldots x_n.M \;\equiv\; \lambda\vec{x}.M \;\equiv\; (\lambda x_1(\ldots(\lambda x_n M)\ldots))$$

where $\vec{x}$ is our notation for the sequence $x_1, \ldots, x_n$. We will generally use the symbol $\equiv$ to denote syntactic equality between terms.

The symbol λ acts as a variable binder in a similar fashion to $\int \ldots dx$ in integral calculus and the quantifiers $\exists$ and $\forall$ in predicate calculus. The set of bound variables is defined inductively by the following function, $BV :\Lambda \to \wp(Var)^3$:

$$\begin{aligned}
BV\,x &= \emptyset \\
BV\,(\lambda x M) &= (BV\,M) \cup \{x\} \\
BV\,(MN) &= (BV\,M) \cup (BV\,N)
\end{aligned}$$

We will also often need to talk about the set of free variables in a term; these are defined inductively by the following function, $FV : \Lambda \to \wp(Var)$:

$$\begin{aligned}
FV\,x &= x \\
FV\,(\lambda x M) &= (FV\,M) - \{x\} \\
FV\,(MN) &= (FV\,M) \cup (FV\,N)
\end{aligned}$$

When $(FV\,M)$ is the empty set, $\emptyset$, M is said to be *closed*; closed terms are sometimes called *combinators* and the class of all such terms is Λ^0. Notice that the sets of bound and free variables are not necessarily disjoint; x occurs both bound and free in:

$$x(\lambda xy.x)$$

Terms which are defined by clause 3 of the definition correspond to applications. We adopt the convention that application is left associative. Consequently:

$$M N_1 \ldots N_n \;\equiv\; M\vec{N} \;\equiv\; (\ldots(MN_1)\ldots N_n)$$

In the following, we also make use of the notion of subterm. A *subterm* of a λ-term is some part of the term which is itself a well-formed λ-term;

---

[2]The λ-terms and the LISP program are type-free. This is in contrast to the PASCAL procedure which is strongly (monomorphically) typed. Both the λ-term and the LISP program are actually equivalent to a whole set of PASCAL procedures with an element for every type.

[3]$f : A \to B$ means that f is a function which takes arguments from the "set" A to results in B. The notation $\wp(A)$ constructs the powerset of A.

we can generate the set of subterms using the function, $Sub : \Lambda \to \wp(\Lambda)$, defined as follows:

$$
\begin{aligned}
Sub\,x &= \{x\} \\
Sub\,(\lambda x M) &= (Sub\,M) \cup \{(\lambda x M)\} \\
Sub\,(MN) &= (Sub\,M) \cup (Sub\,N) \cup \{(MN)\}
\end{aligned}
$$

Notice that the definition of Sub is inductive (recursive) and follows the definition of the syntax of λ-terms. Our definition does not distinguish between different occurrences of the same subterm; to do so we would need to construct a multi-set of subterms but we will not require this refinement in the following.

When we want to prove something about terms we will often use the technique of *structural induction*. A proof by structural induction has a very similar structure to a proof by mathematical induction (see Chapter 1). The basis consists of a demonstration that the predicate holds for each of the primitive terms and the inductive step includes a separate case for each type of composite term in the language using a hypothesis which states that the predicate is true for the immediate subterms of the composite term. To be more concrete, we give an example of a property of λ-terms:

Example 2.3 *Every term in Λ has balanced parentheses*

Proof
Basis:
(i) Variables — trivial since variables contain no parentheses

Inductive Step:
Consider the application (MN). By the inductive hypothesis twice, we have that both M and N are balanced. Then (MN) is also balanced.

Consider the abstraction $(\lambda x.M)$. By the inductive hypothesis we have that M is balanced. Thus $(\lambda x.M)$ is also balanced. $\square$

We conclude this section by defining the class of λ-contexts. Often, we will need the notion of a partially specified term, that is a term with "holes" in it. Such a term gives a context into which we can put other terms (to fill the holes!). The ability to construct contexts will clarify some definitions (for example the notion of *compatibility* used in Chapter 3) and generalise some results (for example see the generalisation of the Substitution Lemma later in this chapter). We give an inductive definition of contexts for λ-terms:

Definition 2.4 (Contexts)
The class $\mathcal{C}[]$ of λ-contexts is the least class satisfying:

(1) $x \in \mathcal{C}[]$
(2) $[] \in \mathcal{C}[]$
(3) *if $C_1[], C_2[] \in \mathcal{C}[]$ then $(C_1[]C_2[]), (\lambda x C_1[]) \in \mathcal{C}[]$*

Notice that a hole is represented by []. An example of a context is:

$$((\lambda x.[]x)M)$$

which is equivalent to (omitting redundant brackets):

$$(\lambda x.[]x)M$$

We will often give a name to a context, say $C[]$ for the one above, such names will always terminate with "[]". To represent the term generated by filling the holes in a context with some term, we write the name of the context with the term that is to fill the hole appearing between the square brackets. Thus:

$$C[\lambda y.y]$$

is the term:

$$(\lambda x.(\lambda y.y)x)M$$

Of course, a context may have many holes but they will all be filled with the same term; we could generalise this by labelling holes, in which case different holes could be filled by different terms, but we will not need such generality in this book.

Notice that variables in $FV(M)$ might become bound in $C[M]$.

2.2   The theory λ

We can construct formulae from the terms; a theory then establishes certain formulae as axioms and provides rules of inference which enable us to derive new formulae. The true formulae (either axioms or formulae that can be derived from the rules) are called *theorems*.

In the standard theory of propositional calculus, the formulae are wff; the theory has three axiom schemes and one rule of inference which is called *Modus Ponens*. In general, each rule of inference has a set of premises, $p_1, \ldots, p_n$, and a conclusion, c. We will write rules in the following way:

$$\frac{p_1 \quad \cdots \quad p_n}{c}$$

The meaning of such a rule is that if all of the premises are theorems then so is the conclusion. The theory of the propositional calculus is thus:

Axiom Schema 1: $((A \vee A) \Rightarrow A)$
Axiom Schema 2: $(A \Rightarrow (B \vee A))$
Axiom Schema 3: $((A \Rightarrow B) \Rightarrow ((C \vee A) \Rightarrow (B \vee C)))$
Modus Ponens: $\dfrac{A \quad A \Rightarrow B}{B}$

Equipped with the theory, we can now generate some new theorems.

Example 2.5 $p \lor \neg p$

Proof

$(p \lor p) \Rightarrow p$	by **Axiom Schema 1**
$((p \lor p) \Rightarrow p) \Rightarrow$	
$((\neg p \lor (p \lor p)) \Rightarrow (p \lor \neg p))$	by **Axiom Schema 3**
$(\neg p \lor (p \lor p)) \Rightarrow (p \lor \neg p)$	by **Modus Ponens**
$p \lor \neg p$	since $\neg p \lor (p \lor p) \equiv p \Rightarrow (p \lor p)$
	use **Axiom Schema 2**
	and **Modus Ponens**

$\square$

We now present a theory of equality (or *convertibility*) between λ-terms. There are a number of reasonable requirements for such a theory:

(1) An application term should be equal to the result obtained by applying the function part of the term to the argument. For example, suspending your knowledge of PASCAL, imagine that PASCAL procedures can be higher-order (take procedures as arguments and produce them as results) and that we have defined a higher-order variant of id. Then:

`id(fun)`

should surely be the same function as `fun` (for any appropriate procedure parameter `fun`).

(2) Equality should be an equivalence relation.

(3) Equal terms should be equal in any context.

These requirements go some way to motivating the following theory, λ:

$$(\lambda x.M)N = M[x := N] \qquad (\beta)$$

$$M = M$$

$$\frac{M = N}{N = M}$$

$$\frac{M = N \quad N = L}{M = L}$$

$$\frac{M = N}{MZ = NZ}$$

$$\frac{M = N}{ZM = ZN}$$

$$\frac{M = N}{\lambda x.M = \lambda x.N} \qquad (\xi)$$

The rule (ξ) is sometimes called the rule of weak extensionality. The rule (β) is the rule which corresponds to function application. The notation $M[x := N]$ should be read "replace free occurrences of x in M by N" (some care must be taken — we return to this in the next section). The classical presentation of the theory also includes an α-rule which allows a change of bound variable names; see the next section for a discussion of this. Readers should compare the rule (β) to their intuitive understanding of the meaning of procedure calls in a familiar programming language.

We write:

$$\lambda \vdash M = N$$

to mean that $M = N$ is a theorem of λ and read the theorem as "M and N are convertible". The notation of the last section and this theory are variously called the λ-calculus (the name that we will use in the following), the $\lambda\beta$-calculus, the λK-calculus or the $\lambda K\beta$-calculus.

Note that:

$$M \equiv N \Rightarrow M = N$$

but:

$$\neg(M = N \Rightarrow M \equiv N)$$

For example:

$$(\lambda x.x)y = y$$

but the two terms are not identical.

Finally, we illustrate the use of the theory to prove a fundamental theorem, the Fixed Point Theorem:

Theorem 2.6 (The Fixed Point Theorem)

$$\forall F \in \Lambda, \exists X \in \Lambda.FX = X$$

Proof
Let $W \equiv \lambda x.F(xx)$ and $X \equiv WW$. Then

$$X \equiv WW \equiv (\lambda x.F(xx))W = F(WW) \equiv FX$$

$\square$

X is called a *fixed point* of F; if we apply F to X, the resulting term is convertible with X. In a more familiar context, for example, 1 is a fixed point of the squaring function. The Fixed Point Theorem may seem quite surprising at first sight; it says that all terms have fixed points. For some terms, such as:

$$\lambda x.x$$

which is the identity function, this is obvious (all terms are fixed points of the identity!) but for others, such as:

$$\lambda xy.xy$$

it is not so clear. However, the proof of the Fixed Point Theorem is constructive; it gives a recipe for constructing a fixed point of any term. In the second case above this leads to the following construction:

$$W \equiv \lambda x.(\lambda xy.xy)(xx) = \lambda x.\lambda y.(xx)y \equiv \lambda xy.(xx)y$$

The required fixed point is thus $(\lambda xy.(xx)y)(\lambda xy.(xx)y)$; we check that this is indeed a fixed point of the original term:

$$(\lambda xy.(xx)y)(\lambda xy.(xx)y)$$
$$= \lambda y.((\lambda xy.(xx)y)(\lambda xy.(xx)y))y$$
$$= (\lambda xy.xy)((\lambda xy.(xx)y)(\lambda xy.(xx)y))$$

The fixed point constructed for the identity function is:

$$(\lambda x.xx)(\lambda x.xx)$$

This term plays a special role in the theory which we shall return to later[4].

Fixed points are important in Computer Science. They play a fundamental role in the semantics of recursive definitions. For example, the factorial function:

---

[4]For those readers familiar with domain theory, this term plays the same role as $\perp$. It is the <u>least</u> fixed point of the identity function (and many others!).

$$fac\ 0\qquad\ \ =1$$
$$fac\ (succ\ n) = (succ\ n) \times (fac\ n)$$

is a fixed point of the term:

$$\lambda fn.if(= n\ 0)\ 1\ (\times n\ (f(pred\ n)))$$

(of course we must be careful about reading too much into this term – $0, 1, \times$ are just formal symbols, variables, they have no deeper significance in the λ-calculus which we have defined so far). We shall return to this point later.

2.3 Substitution

We now return to the substitution operation used in the rule (β). A naive approach to defining this operation leads to the problem of "variable capture". This problem occurs when we naively substitute a term containing a free variable into a scope where the variable becomes bound. For example:

$$(\lambda xy.yx)y \neq \lambda y.yy$$

The free occurrence of y in the left hand term is analogous to a global variable in programming, in the right hand side the global variable has become confused with the bound variable (formal parameter). We will consider three different approaches to this problem before selecting one for use in the rest of this book.

2.3.1 Three Approaches

The Classical Approach

The first approach is based on Church's original treatment of substitution. We use the following definition:

(1) $x[x := N] \equiv N$

(2) $y[x := N] \equiv y$, if x is not the same as y

(3) $(\lambda x.M)[x := N] \equiv \lambda x.M$

(4) $(\lambda y.M)[x := N] \equiv \lambda y.M[x := N]$, if $x \notin FV\ M$ or $y \notin FV\ N$

(5) $(\lambda y.M)[x := N] \equiv \lambda z.(M[y := z])[x := N]$, if $x \in FV\ M$ and $y \in FV\ N$, z a new variable

(6) $(M_1 M_2)[x := N] \equiv (M_1[x := N])(M_2[x := N])$

We consider the three rules 3 to 5 in a bit more detail. Rule 3 applies when the variable being substituted for is bound at the outermost level; in this case there will be no free occurrences of x in the remainder of the expression and thus the substitution has no effect. Rule 4 is applicable when variable capture cannot occur, either x does not occur free in the body (in which case the substitution is a no-operation again) or the variable that is bound in the outermost level does not occur free in the term being substituted (no capture); in either case the substitution can be pushed through the λ to apply to the body. The final rule, 5, applies when variable capture could occur, that is when some substitution does take place and the variable bound at the outermost level does occur free in the term being substituted; in this case, we first rename the bound variable to a completely new variable.

Rule 5 is only valid under the assumption that terms which are similar, having the same free variables and differing only in their bound variables, are essentially the same. This is reasonable if we think about programming languages:

```
FUNCTION id(y:integer):integer;
BEGIN id := y END;
```

the above procedure is clearly the same as the earlier one with the same name; we have only changed the formal parameters. In Church's original presentation of the λ-calculus there were two additional axioms; (α) formalises the above discussion and (η) introduces extensional equality (see below). The alpha rule is:

$$\lambda x.M = \lambda y.M[x := y], y \notin FV\, M \qquad (\alpha)$$

The Variable Convention

For our second definition of the substitution operation, which is introduced in Barendregt's book, we start with two definitions:

Definition 2.7 (Change of Bound Variables)
M' is produced from M by a change of bound variables if $M \equiv C[\lambda x.N]$ and $M' \equiv C[\lambda y.(N[x := y])]$ where y does not occur at all in N and $C[]$ is a context with one hole.

Definition 2.8 (α-congruence)
M is α-congruent to N, written $M \equiv_\alpha N$, if N results from M by a series of changes of bound variable.

According to the second definition, we have:

$$\lambda x.xy \equiv_\alpha \lambda z.zy$$

but not:

$$\lambda x.xy \equiv_\alpha \lambda y.yy$$

Notice that the first two terms are also equal by the rule (α) but the second two are not; indeed the notion of "change of bound variable" is the compatible closure of (α)(see Chapter 3). Our strategy for defining substitution is as follows:

(1) Identify α-congruent terms

(2) Consider a λ-term as a representative of its equivalence class

(3) Interpret $M[x := N]$ as an operation on the equivalence classes, using representatives according to the following *variable convention:*

Definition 2.9 (Variable Convention)

If $M_1, \ldots, M_n$ occur in a certain context then in these terms all bound variables are chosen to be different from free variables[5].

With this strategy, we can define substitution as follows:

(1) $x[x := N] \equiv N$

(2) $y[x := N] \equiv y$, if $x \not\equiv y$

(3) $(\lambda y.M)[x := N] \equiv \lambda y.(M[x := N])$

(4) $(M_1 M_2)[x := N] \equiv (M_1[x := N])(M_2[x := N])$

The variable capture problem has disappeared! — the reason for this is that for y to appear free in N in the context:

$$(\lambda y.M)[x := N]$$

would breach the variable convention so we would have to use a different representative of the α-equivalence class of $\lambda y.M$ (this is precisely what rule 5 in the classical approach makes explicit). In the following, we will adopt this convention and definition of substitution because it is easier to work with (there are less cases to consider in proofs). An example of its use is illustrated below:

$$(\lambda xyz.xzy)(\lambda xz.x) = \lambda yz.(\lambda xw.x)zy \text{ by the variable convention}$$
$$= \lambda yz.(\lambda w.z)y$$
$$= \lambda yz.z$$

However, before continuing we consider a third alternative which will be useful in the definition of abstract machines in Chapter 8.

The de Bruijn Notation

The third approach to defining substitution avoids the problem of variable capture by banishing free variables. We revise the definition of λ-terms so that parameters occurring in the body of a term are referred to by natural numbers which uniquely identify the binding λ. For example:

$$\lambda.\lambda.2$$

is equivalent to:

$$\lambda xy.x$$

---

[5] We have already implicitly employed this convention in the proof of the Fixed Point Theorem — consider what happens if x occurs free in the term F.

This is the notation invented by de Bruijn and used in the Automath project, an automated theorem proving system. More formally the terms in de Bruijn's notation are defined inductively as the least set such that:

(1) any natural number (greater than zero) is a term
(2) If M and N are terms, then (MN) is a term
(3) If M is a term, (λM) is a term

and (β) is replaced by:

$$(\lambda P)Q = P[1 := Q]$$

where:

$$
\begin{aligned}
n[m := N] \quad &\equiv n \text{ if } n < m \\
&\quad n - 1 \text{ if } n > m \\
&\quad rename_{n,1}(N) \text{ if } n = m \\
(M_1 M_2)[m := N] &\equiv (M_1[m := N])(M_2[m := N]) \\
(\lambda M)[m := N] \quad &\equiv \lambda(M[m + 1 := N])
\end{aligned}
$$

and

$$
\begin{aligned}
rename_{m,i}(j) \quad &\equiv j \text{ if } j < i \\
&\quad j + m - 1 \text{ if } j \geq i \\
rename_{m,i}(N_1 N_2) &\equiv rename_{m,i}(N_1)rename_{m,i}(N_2) \\
rename_{m,i}(\lambda N) \quad &\equiv \lambda(rename_{m,i+1}(N))
\end{aligned}
$$

The reader should take care to check that this new beta rule has the same effect as the earlier version. For example:

Example 2.10
$$
\begin{aligned}
\lambda.(\lambda.\lambda.2)1 &= \lambda.(\lambda.2)[1 := 1] \\
&\equiv \lambda.\lambda.2[2 := 1] \\
&\equiv \lambda.\lambda.rename_{2,1}(1) \\
&\equiv \lambda.\lambda.2
\end{aligned}
$$
c.f. $(\lambda x.(\lambda yz.y)x)$

Notice the rôle that rename takes in relabelling variable indices. There is a simple translation between standard λ-terms and de Bruijn terms (notice that α-congruent terms are equal in the de Bruijn notation):

$$
\begin{aligned}
DB\,x\,(x_1,\ldots,x_n) \quad &= i, \text{ if } i \text{ is the minimum such that } x \equiv x_i \\
DB\,(\lambda x M)\,(x_1,\ldots,x_n) &= \lambda(DB\,M\,(x,x_1,\ldots,x_n)) \\
DB\,(MN)\,(x_1,\ldots,x_n) &= (DB\,M\,(x_1,\ldots,x_n))(DB\,N\,(x_1,\ldots,x_n))
\end{aligned}
$$

The de Bruijn notation is not very readable but the beta rule is easy to implement; indeed it inspired the Categorical Abstract Machine — an efficient mechanism for the implementation of functional languages; we will return to this later. However most treatments of the de Bruijn notation present it formally and then use standard λ-terms wherever possible.

2.3.2 The Substitution Lemma

From now on, we will assume the variable convention unless otherwise stated.

We now present a result which allows us to reorder substitutions, The Substitution Lemma:

Lemma 2.11 (The Substitution Lemma)
If x and y are distinct variables and $x \notin FV\ L$ then

$$M[x := N][y := L] \equiv M[y := L][x := N[y := L]]$$

Proof
(by induction on the structure of M)

(i) If M is a variable there are three cases to consider:
  If $M \equiv x$ then both sides $\equiv N[y := L]$ since x is distinct from y
  If $M \equiv y$ then both sides $\equiv L$ since $x \notin FV\ L$
  If $M \equiv z$ where z is distinct from both x and y, then both sides $\equiv z$

(ii) If $M \equiv \lambda z.M_1$ then, by the variable convention, z is distinct from x and y and $z \notin FV\ NL$ and:

$$(\lambda z.M_1)[x := N][y := L] \equiv \lambda z.M_1[x := N][y := L]$$
$$\text{by defn. of substitution}$$
$$\equiv \lambda z.M_1[y := L][x := N[y := L]] \text{ by IH}$$
$$\equiv (\lambda z.M_1)[y := L][x := N[y := L]]$$
$$\text{by defn. of substitution}$$

(iii) If $M \equiv M_1 M_2$ then:

$$(M_1 M_2)[x := N][y := L] \equiv (M_1[x := N][y := L])(M_2[x := N][y := L])$$
$$\text{by defn. of substitution}$$
$$\equiv (M_1[y := L][x := N[y := L]])$$
$$(M_2[y := L][x := N[y := L]])$$
$$\text{by IH twice}$$
$$\equiv (M_1 M_2)[y := L][x := N[y := L]]$$
$$\text{by defn. of substitution}$$

$\square$

Exercise 2.3.1 *Formulate and prove the substitution lemma for de Bruijn's notation*

Lemma 2.12 *Substitution has a number of other useful properties with respect to convertibility:*
  (1) $M = M' \Rightarrow M[x := N] = M'[x := N]$
  (2) $N = N' \Rightarrow M[x := N] = M[x := N']$

(3) $M = M', N = N' \Rightarrow M[x := N] = M'[x := N']$

Proof
(1) $M = M' \Rightarrow \lambda x.M = \lambda x.M'$ by (ξ)
$\Rightarrow (\lambda x.M)N = (\lambda x.M')N$
$\Rightarrow M[x := N] = M'[x := N]$ by (β) twice

(2) see exercise

(3) follows directly from (1) and (2):
$M = M' \Rightarrow M[x := N] = M'[x := N]$ by (1)
$N = N' \Rightarrow M'[x := N] = M'[x := N']$ by (2)
Thus $M[x := N] = M'[x := N']$ by transitivity of $=$ $\qquad\square$

An alternative proof of the first result uses a new proof technique: induction over the length of a proof. The length of a proof is the number of steps taken to derive a formula; if the formula is an axiom then the length is zero, otherwise it is 1 plus the lengths of proofs of all of the premises used in the last step of the proof (which has the formula as its conclusion). The basis of the proof considers the axioms and the inductive step has a case for each of the inference rules.

Exercise 2.3.2 *a. Construct a proof of (1) by induction over the length of the proof of $M = M'$ (Hint: you may have to use the Substitution Lemma) b. Construct a proof of (2) by structural induction.*

These properties are useful but care should be taken when applying them. A major property of functional languages is *referential transparency*; the property which allows equals to be substituted by equals. The properties of substitution appear to be related to this concept but referential transparency is more. For example, the following inference does not follow from (1) to (3):

$$N = N' \Rightarrow \lambda x.x(\lambda y.N) = \lambda x.x(\lambda y.N')$$

This is because we cannot express the two sides of the second equality in the correct form:

$$\lambda x.x(\lambda y.N) \text{ is not the same as } (\lambda x.x(\lambda y.z))[z := N]$$

since N may contain free occurrences of y. The correct formulation of the property of referential transparency, also referred to as Leibniz' Law, is:

Lemma 2.13 (Referential Transparency)
Let $C[]$ be a context, then

$$N = N' \Rightarrow C[N] = C[N']$$

Proof
(by induction on the structure of $C[]$)

$C[] \equiv x :$ then $C[N] \equiv x \equiv C[N']$

$C[] \equiv [] : C[N] \equiv N = N'$(by the assumption) $\equiv C[N']$

$C[] \equiv C_1[]C_2[] :$

$$\begin{aligned} C[N] &\equiv C_1[N]C_2[N] \\ &= C_1[N']C_2[N] \text{ by IH and } \lambda \\ &= C_1[N']C_2[N'] \text{ by IH and } \lambda \\ &\equiv C[N'] \end{aligned}$$

$C[] \equiv \lambda x.C_1[] :$

$$\begin{aligned} C[N] &\equiv \lambda x.C_1[N] \\ &= \lambda x.C_1[N'] \text{ by IH and } (\xi) \\ &\equiv C[N'] \end{aligned}$$

$\square$

2.4 Extensionality

The convertibility relationship, $=$, is intensional equality; two terms are equal if they encode the same algorithm in some sense. This does not equate some terms which we might naturally think of as equal. For example, consider a term which has one bound variable and applies some constant term (i.e. a term that does not contain free occurrences of the bound variable) to any term bound to the variable:

$$\lambda x.Mx$$

this term should surely be equal to M since if we apply either $\lambda x.Mx$ or M to some term N, we end up with MN. This is the classical notion of extensional equality discussed in Chapter 1. The formula:

$$\lambda x.Mx = M$$

is not a theorem of λ; there are two ways we can extend λ to make the above formula a theorem. Firstly, we could add a new rule to the theory, giving the new theory $\lambda + ext :$

$$\frac{Mx = Nx}{M = N} \qquad x \notin (FV \ MN) \qquad\qquad \textbf{(ext)}$$

Alternatively, we can add a new axiom, giving the new theory $\lambda\eta$ (as proposed by Church):

$$\lambda x.Mx = M, x \notin FV \ M \qquad (\eta)$$

In fact, we have the following result:

Lemma 2.14 $\lambda + \textbf{ext}$ *and* $\lambda\eta$ *are equivalent*

Proof

$\lambda + \text{ext} \vdash \lambda x.Mx = M, x \notin FV\,M$:

Since $(\lambda x.Mx)x = Mx$ by (β) then if $x \notin FV\,M, (\lambda x.Mx) = M$ by **ext**

$\lambda\eta \vdash \text{ext}$:

Assume $Mx = Nx$ with $x \notin FV\,MN$ then $\lambda x.Mx = \lambda x.Nx$ by (ξ) and hence by (η) twice, we have $M = N$ □

The calculus based on $\lambda\eta$ or $\lambda + \text{ext}$ is alternatively called the $\lambda\eta$-calculus, the $\lambda\beta\eta$-calculus, the $\lambda K\eta$-calculus or the $\lambda K\beta\eta$-calculus. Practically, from the point of view of functional programming, the $\lambda\eta$-calculus is not as important as the $\lambda\beta$-calculus since the rule (η) is not normally implemented (see Peyton Jones, for example, for a discussion of this point). The term $\lambda x.Mx$ is a weak head normal form (see Chapters 8 and 9) and is thus distinguishable from M; the former is a "value" the latter may lead to a non-terminating computation. Even in an eager language, such as Standard ML, the two terms are distinguished. However, the $\lambda\eta$-calculus does have some theoretical significance which we shall return to later.

2.5   Consistency and Completeness

For a theory to be useful, there must be some theorems and not all closed formulae should be theorems. The former is satisfied provided that the theory has at least one axiom. The latter is slightly trickier and is quite a fragile property; a theory which satisfies this constraint is called *consistent*. Both of the theories presented here are consistent but it is very easy to lose consistency as we shall see.

We start by formalising the concept. First, some definitions:

Definition 2.15 *An* equation *is a formula of the form:*

$$M = N$$

where $M, N \in \Lambda$.

Definition 2.16 *An equation is* closed *if* $M, N \in \Lambda^0$.

Definition 2.17 (Consistency)
If $\mathcal{T}$ *is a theory with equations as formulae then* $\mathcal{T}$ *is* consistent, *written* $Con(\mathcal{T})$, *if it does not prove every closed equation.*
If $\mathcal{T}$ *is a set of equations then* $\lambda + \mathcal{T}$ *is formed by adding the equations of* $\mathcal{T}$ *as axioms to* λ. $\mathcal{T}$ *is consistent, also written* $Con(\mathcal{T})$, *if* $Con(\lambda + \mathcal{T})$.

Both of the theories that we have dealt with in this Chapter, λ and $\lambda\eta$ are consistent (see Barendregt's book). The property of consistency is fairly fragile; it can be disturbed by adding a single equation. We define the following three terms:

$$\mathbf{S} \equiv \lambda xyz.xz(yz)$$

$$\mathbf{K} \equiv \lambda xy.x$$

$$\mathbf{I} \equiv \lambda x.x$$

Notice that:

$$\mathbf{S}MNO = MO(NO) \text{ by three applications of } (\beta)$$

$$\mathbf{K}MN = M$$

$$\mathbf{I}M = M$$

Now, if we add the equation:

$$\mathbf{S} = \mathbf{K}$$

to either λ or $\lambda\eta$ we get an inconsistent theory. This can be proved as follows (we elide some of the steps):

Example 2.18
$$\mathbf{S} = \mathbf{K} \quad \Rightarrow \quad \mathbf{S}ABC = \mathbf{K}ABC \text{ for all } A, B, C$$
$$\Rightarrow \quad AC(BC) = AC$$
Now consider the case when $A = C = \mathbf{I}$, then since $\mathbf{I}A = A$ for all A:
$$AC(BC) = AC \Rightarrow B(\mathbf{I}) = \mathbf{I}$$
Now consider the case when $B = \mathbf{K}D$ for some arbitrary D, then:
$$B(\mathbf{I}) = \mathbf{I} \Rightarrow D = \mathbf{I}$$
and thus, since D was arbitrary, all terms are equal to the constant term $\mathbf{I}$.

The reader should redo this proof, filling in the missing steps and justifications.

Consideration of the foregoing motivates the following definition:

Definition 2.19 (Incompatibility)
Let $M, N \in \Lambda$, then M and N are incompatible, written $M \# N$, if $\neg Con(M = N)$.

This notion of incompatibility leads to a useful proof technique as exemplified by the following example and exercise. The basic proof technique is as follows:

- Use weak extensionality to generate a closed equation.
- Apply both sides of the equation to the same distinct, arbitrary terms $(M, N, O \ldots)$, equal in number to the largest number of outermost $\lambda's$ on either side of the equation.
- Perform β-conversions.

- Set the arbitrary terms to specific constants $(\mathbf{I}, \mathbf{K} \ldots)$ and try to derive an equation:

$$arbitrary\ term = constant$$

This technique is illustrated by the following example:

Example 2.20 $xx \# xy$

Proof

Assume that $xx = xy$; then:

	$\lambda xy.xx$	$=$	$\lambda xy.xy$	by weak extensionality twice
$\Rightarrow$	$(\lambda xy.xx)MN$	$=$	$(\lambda xy.xy)MN$	for arbitrary M, N
$\Rightarrow$	MM	$=$	MN	by β twice
$\Rightarrow$	$\mathbf{I}$	$=$	N	choosing $M \equiv \mathbf{I}$

□

Exercise 2.5.1

Show that application is not associative by proving that:

$$x(yz) \# (xy)z$$

We now turn to the notion of completeness. Yet again, we start by making some definitions:

Definition 2.21 (Normal Forms)

If $M \in \Lambda$, then M is a β-normal form, written β-nf or nf, if M has no subterms of the form $(\lambda x.R)S$

If $M \in \Lambda$, then M has a β-nf if there exists an N such that $N = M$ and N is a β-nf.

Some (non-)examples of normal forms:

$$\lambda x.x \text{ is a nf}$$

$$(\lambda xy.x)(\lambda x.x) \text{ has } \lambda yx.x \text{ as a nf}$$

$$(\lambda x.xx)(\lambda x.xx) \text{ does not have a nf}$$

By analogy, a $\beta\eta$-nf is a β-nf which also does not contain any subterms of the form:

$$(\lambda x.Rx) \text{ with } x \notin FV\ R$$

We now state the following facts about normal forms:

Proposition 2.22

(1) *M has a $\beta\eta$-nf $\Leftrightarrow$ M has a β-nf*

(2) *If M and N are distinct β-nfs then M = N is not a theorem of λ(and similarly for λη).*

(3) *If M and N are distinct βη-nfs then M#N.*

The proof of this proposition requires considerable extra machinery which goes beyond the scope of this book; the interested reader is referred to Chapter 2 of Barendregt's book. The use of $βη$-nfs in the last point is essential; y and $λx.yx$ are distinct $β$-nfs but not incompatible – they are $η$-equivalent.

The completeness of $λη$ is expressed by the following:

Proposition 2.23 (Completeness)
Suppose M and N have nfs; then either:
$$λη ⊢ M = N$$
or
$$λη + (M = N) \text{ is inconsistent}$$

2.6 Summary

We have now completed our treatment of $λ$-conversion, the $=$ relation defined by $λ$. The reader is urged to refer to Barendregt's book for an encyclopaedic treatment of this topic.

The convertibility relation, being an equivalence relation, partitions the class of $λ$-terms. When dealing with equivalence classes, it is convenient to use canonical representatives. The obvious representatives to use in our study of the $λ$-calculus are the normal forms (take care — what about the terms, such as $(λx.xx)(λx.xx)$, which have no normal form? If we equate them we get an inconsistent theory (see later)). In the next chapter, we will study the notion of *reduction*, in which terms are successively simplified towards normal form. The computational motivation for this study is that normal forms equate to "answers" and thus the process of reduction is the familiar notion of evaluation used in functional programming languages.

3

Reduction

Overview

Convertibility is a symmetric relation and therefore does not correspond very closely to our intuitions about computing with terms. In this chapter we study a new relation on terms which better fits our intuitions. Having introduced the basic concepts, we present the Church–Rosser Theorem; this is a central theorem in the λ-calculus and we study it in some detail. The other key theorem is the Standardisation Theorem; before presenting this we require the notion of a *residual* and a definition of *head normal forms*. We also show how constants may be added to the calculus and establish conditions under which the Church–Rosser property is preserved.

3.1   Introduction

We have suggested that normal forms should be used as canonical representatives for the convertibility equivalence classes. A more computational view results from treating normal forms as the "answers" produced from λ-term "programs". This view is justified by observing that the evaluation of the β-normal form of a term involves removing application subterms by applying the (β) rule; we have already identified this process with function application in programming languages. We will pursue this view further[1].

We illustrate the earlier discussion and motivate the following material by considering an example in a λ-calculus extended with constants. We consider the following program:

```
let
fac 0 = 1
fac n = n * fac(n-1)
in fac 0
```

We briefly discussed a variant of this function in the last chapter, where we saw that it was the fixed point of a certain functional. We consider that the calculus which we are using is extended with a constant, **Y**, which computes the fixed point of a given term; following the construction used

---

[1] Notice that in lazy functional languages such as Haskell, rather than normal forms, (weak) head normal forms are considered to be answers — we shall return to this point later.

in the proof of the Fixed Point Theorem, it is clear that such a constant could be defined by the following term:

$$\lambda f.((\lambda x.f(xx))(\lambda x.f(xx)))$$

The program may be translated in the following way:

$$(\lambda f.f0)(\mathbf{Y}(\lambda fn.if(= n\ 0)1(* n\ (f(- n\ 1))))))$$

notice that the let-construct has been translated as an application term.

Consider now the normal form of the program. We can produce the normal form by repeatedly applying rule (β); in outline, we perform the following steps[2]:

$$
\begin{aligned}
(\lambda f.f0)(\mathbf{Y}\ldots) &= (\mathbf{Y}\ldots)0 \\
&= (\lambda fn.if\ldots)(\mathbf{Y}\ldots)0 & (A) \\
&= (\lambda n.if(= n\ 0)1(*n((\mathbf{Y}\ldots)(- n\ 1))))0 \\
&= if(= 0\ 0)1(*0((\mathbf{Y}\ldots)(- 0\ 1))) \\
&= if\ \mathbf{true}\ 1\ldots \\
&= 1
\end{aligned}
$$

Throughout this derivation we have used the convertibility relation introduced in the last chapter. Convertibility is symmetrical, indeed it is an equivalence relation, but we have used it in a non-symmetrical way. We are happy to consider 1 as the answer of the above computation, the factorial of 0, but it is a little harder to see the original program as the value of the term "1". The latter view would associate an infinite set of "values" with terms such as "1". In this chapter, we will study some new relations between λ-terms, notably $\to_\beta$ (one step β-reduction) and $\twoheadrightarrow_\beta$ (β-reduction), the reflexive, transitive closure of $\to_\beta$. We will see that $\twoheadrightarrow_\beta$ is closely related to $=$ but is not symmetric; each $=$ in the above derivation, other than the one in step (A), could be replaced by $\to_\beta$.

In performing reduction, we are faced with a problem of strategy. For example, at line (A) there are two subterms of the form $(\lambda x.R)S$ — henceforth called β-redexes (**red**ucible **ex**pression) — as follows:

$$(\lambda fn.if\ldots)(\mathbf{Y}\ldots)0$$

and

$$(\mathbf{Y}\ldots)$$

that is, the whole term and the subterm involving the fixed point combinator. We chose to reduce the first term but consider what would happen

---

[2]We have elided two steps here and used a defining property of fixed point combinators such as $\mathbf{Y}$:

$$\mathbf{Y}F = F(\mathbf{Y}F)$$

if we consistently chose to reduce the fixed point subterm: we would never get to the answer, we would merely construct a larger and larger term! Making the "wrong" choice is not always so catastrophic, for example:

$$(\lambda xy./(+\ x\ y)2)((\lambda z. +\ z\ 1)4)6 \to_\beta (\lambda y./(+((\lambda z. +\ z\ 1)4)y)2)6$$
$$\to_\beta /(+((\lambda z. +\ z\ 1)4)6)2$$
$$\to_\beta /(+(+\ 4\ 1)6)2$$

but also:

$$(\lambda xy./(+\ x\ y)2)((\lambda z. +\ z\ 1)4)6 \to_\beta (\lambda xy./(+\ x\ y)2)(+\ 4\ 1)6$$
$$\to_\beta (\lambda y./(+(+\ 4\ 1)y)2)6$$
$$\to_\beta /(+(+\ 4\ 1)6)2$$

and so the answer will be the same.

Exercise 3.1.1 *There are some other reduction sequences leading from the above term; write them down. Invent some other terms and write down the various reduction sequences from the chosen terms.*

The above discussion should pose two questions in the reader's mind:

Question 1: Given a term and a number of reduction sequences from that term which all terminate in a normal form, is it possible that some of the sequences might terminate with different normal forms?

Question 2: Given that some choices of reduction strategy appear to be better than others in some situations (for example the bottomless pit of $(\mathbf{Y} \ldots))$ is there a best way of choosing what to do next?

The first question is closely related to the issue of *determinacy*; computationally, the question amounts to asking if we can get different answers from a program depending on how we execute it. A corollary of the Church–Rosser Theorem, which we will present below, guarantees that the answer to this question is no. The second question is less precisely formulated; the Standardisation Theorem, also presented below, addresses the question by giving a reduction order which is guaranteed to terminate with normal form if any reduction sequence does (recall $(\lambda x.xx)(\lambda x.xx)!$) but if "best" is also meant to be read as "optimal" then the question is more complicated — see the references for a more detailed discussion of this topic.

3.2 Notions of Reduction

Reduction may be viewed as a special form of relation on λ-terms. Why special? Recall the discussion of the constraints on equality in Chapter 2; it is reasonable to place some of the same constraints on reduction. For example, if one term reduces to another, then it should do so in any context. On the other hand, bearing in mind our earlier discussion, we should not expect a reduction relation to be an equivalence. We make the following definitions:

Definition 3.1 $R \subseteq \Lambda^2$ *is* compatible *if:*

$$(M, M') \in R \Rightarrow (C[M], C[M']) \in R$$

for all $M, M' \in \Lambda$ and all contexts $C[]$ with one hole.

Definition 3.2 $R \subseteq \Lambda^2$, *is an* equality (congruence) *relation if it is a compatible equivalence relation.*

Definition 3.3 $R \subseteq \Lambda^2$, *is a* reduction *relation if it is compatible, reflexive and transitive.*

Later, in Chapters 8 and 9, we will see that there are sometimes good reasons for relaxing the compatibility requirement.

We now turn to describing how a one-step reduction relation, a reduction relation and an equality relation can be defined from a basic relation. The basic technique is to take closures of the given set; to make a set satisfy some property, we add elements, in an appropriate way, until the set does satisfy the property. For example, consider a subset of $A \times A$ for some set A; to make the subset a reflexive relation on A, for all $a \in A$ we add the pair (a, a) - this generates the reflexive closure of the original subset.

We call an arbitrary binary relation on Λ, a *notion of reduction*. For example, the notion of reduction that we will be particularly interested in is:

$$\beta = \{((\lambda x.M)N, M[x := N]) \mid M, N \in \Lambda\}$$

Given two notions of reduction, R_1 and R_2, we sometimes write $R_1 R_2$ for $R_1 \cup R_2$ (notably in the case that R_1 is β and R_2 is η, we write $\beta\eta$).

The one-step reduction relation induced by some notion of reduction R, written $\rightarrow_R$, is the compatible closure of R. The closure is explicitly constructed as follows:

Definition 3.4 (One-step R-reduction)

$$\frac{(M, N) \in R}{M \rightarrow_R N}$$

$$\frac{M \rightarrow_R N}{MZ \rightarrow_R NZ}$$

$$\frac{M \rightarrow_R N}{ZM \rightarrow_R ZN}$$

$$\frac{M \rightarrow_R N}{\lambda x.M \rightarrow_R \lambda x.N}$$

The notation "$M \rightarrow_R N$" should be read as "M R-reduces to N in one step" or "N is an R-reduct of M". We have already seen the relation $\rightarrow_\beta$, in this case we will often say that "M reduces to N in one step" or "N is a reduct of M".

The reduction relation, written $\twoheadrightarrow_R$, is the reflexive, transitive closure of the one-step reduction relation. While, as its name implies, the one-step reduction relation allows a single step of reduction, the reduction relation allows many (including zero! — allowed by reflexivity). The reflexive transitive closure is defined formally as follows:

Definition 3.5 (R-reduction)

$$\frac{M \rightarrow_R N}{M \twoheadrightarrow_R N}$$

$$M \twoheadrightarrow_R M$$

$$\frac{M \twoheadrightarrow_R N \quad N \twoheadrightarrow_R L}{M \twoheadrightarrow_R L}$$

For the notation "$M \twoheadrightarrow_R N$", read "M R-reduces to N".

Finally, we consider R-equality (also called R-convertibility), written $=_R$. This is the equivalence relation generated by $\twoheadrightarrow_R$. To generate the equivalence relation, we must take the symmetric closure of the relation. But care must be taken; given some reflexive and transitive relation over $\{1, 2, 3\}$, say:

$$\{(1,1), (2,2), (3,3), (1,2), (1,3)\}$$

the symmetric closure:

$$\{(1,1), (2,2), (3,3), (1,2), (1,3), (2,1), (3,1)\}$$

is no longer transitive, we need to add the following elements to restore transitivity:

$$(3, 2) \text{ and } (2, 3)$$

Thus, in general, having taken the symmetric closure, it is necessary to then take the transitive closure:

Definition 3.6 (R-convertibility)

$$\frac{M \twoheadrightarrow_R N}{M =_R N}$$

$$\frac{M =_R N}{N =_R M}$$

$$\frac{M =_R N \quad N =_R L}{M =_R L}$$

In the case that "$M =_R N$", we say "M is R-convertible to N".

We have the following result for these relations:

Proposition 3.7 $\to_R$, $\twoheadrightarrow_R$ *and* $=_R$ *are all compatible.*

Proof
For $\to_R$, the proof is immediate from the definition.
For $\twoheadrightarrow_R$ and $=_R$ the proof is by induction on the definition. Since we have not seen this form of induction before, we illustrate the proof for $\twoheadrightarrow_R$:

Basis:
$M \twoheadrightarrow_R N$ because $M \to_R N$, then since $\to_R$ is compatible $C[M] \to_R C[N]$ and thus $C[M] \twoheadrightarrow_R C[N]$.

$M \twoheadrightarrow_R N$ because $M \equiv N$, then the proof is trivial.

Inductive Step:
$M \twoheadrightarrow_R N$ is a consequence of $M \twoheadrightarrow_R L$ and $L \twoheadrightarrow_R N$, then $C[M] \twoheadrightarrow_R C[L]$ by the IH and $C[L] \twoheadrightarrow_R C[N]$ by the IH and thus:

$$C[M] \twoheadrightarrow_R C[N]$$

$\square$

Earlier, we discussed substitution and presented some results which related $=$ to the substitution operation (notably the Substitution Lemma). Similar considerations applied to $\to_R$ and $\twoheadrightarrow_R$ help us establish some differences between the two.

Lemma 3.8 $N \twoheadrightarrow_R N' \Rightarrow M[x := N] \twoheadrightarrow_R M[x := N']$

Proof
Follows from an induction on the structure of M and the compatibility of $\twoheadrightarrow_R$:

Basis:
$M \equiv z$, z any variable: trivial

Inductive Step:
$M \equiv M_1 M_2$:

$$
\begin{aligned}
M[x := N] \;\equiv\;& M_1[x := N]M_2[x := N] \\
\twoheadrightarrow_R\;& M_1[x := N']M_2[x := N] \text{ by IH and compatibility of } \twoheadrightarrow_R \\
\twoheadrightarrow_R\;& M_1[x := N']M_2[x := N'] \text{ by IH and compatibility of } \twoheadrightarrow_R \\
\equiv\;& M[x := N']
\end{aligned}
$$

$M \equiv \lambda y.M'$:

$$M[x := N] \equiv (\lambda y.M')[x := N]$$
$$\equiv \lambda y.M'[x := N]$$
$$\twoheadrightarrow_R \lambda y.M'[x := N'] \quad \text{by IH and compatibility of } \twoheadrightarrow_R$$
$$\equiv M[x := N']$$

$\square$

The same result does not hold for $\rightarrow_R$, since the substitution may cause redexes (see below) to be duplicated. For example consider: $M \equiv xx$, $N \equiv (\lambda y.y)z$ and $N' \equiv z$, then:

$$N \rightarrow_R N'$$

but:

$$(\lambda y.y)z((\lambda y.y)z) \not\rightarrow_R zz$$

Definition 3.9 *An R-redex is a term M such that $(M, N) \in R$ for some term N; in this case N is called an R-contractum of M. A term M is called an R-normal form (R-nf) if it does not contain any R-redex. A term N is an R-nf of M if N is an R-nf and $M =_R N$.*

We now present a result which gives some constraints on the form of terms which are related by the one-step reduction relation:

Proposition 3.10 $M \rightarrow_R N \Leftrightarrow M \equiv C[P]$, $N \equiv C[Q]$ *and* $(P, Q) \in R$ *for some $P, Q \in \Lambda$ where $C[]$ has one hole.*

Proof

$(\Rightarrow)$
By induction on the definition of $\rightarrow_R$.

$M \rightarrow_R N$ because $(M, N) \in R$: trivial with $C[] = []$.

$M \rightarrow_R N$ because $M \equiv ZS$ and $N \equiv ZT$ and $S \rightarrow_R T$: the IH applies to the reduction from S to T and thus there is a context $C[]$ such that $S \equiv C[P]$ and $T \equiv C[Q]$ with $(P, Q) \in R$. Thus we can take the context $ZC[]$ to complete the proof.

The other cases are similar.

$(\Leftarrow)$
Follows by the compatibility of $\rightarrow_R$.

$\square$

A corollary of this result gives us some, not unexpected, results relating reduction and normal forms:

Corollary 3.2.1 *Let M be an R-nf, then:*

(i) There is no N such that $M \to_R N$

(ii) $M \twoheadrightarrow_R N \Rightarrow M \equiv N$

Proof

(i) by the above result and definition of R-nf.

(ii) by (i), since $\twoheadrightarrow_R$ is the reflexive, transitive closure of $\to_R$. □

Care should be taken with this result; it is not the case that if:

$$\forall N, M \twoheadrightarrow_R N \Rightarrow M \equiv N$$

then M is an R-nf. To see why, consider the following term with R being β:

$$M \equiv (\lambda x.xx)(\lambda x.xx)$$

We are now ready to present the Church–Rosser Theorem.

3.3   The Church–Rosser Theorem

We start by introducing the *diamond property*:

Definition 3.11 (The Diamond Property) *Let $\triangleright$ be a binary relation on Λ, then $\triangleright$ satisfies the diamond property, written $\triangleright \models \Diamond$, if:*

$$\forall M, M_1, M_2 [M \triangleright M_1 \wedge M \triangleright M_2 \Rightarrow \exists M_3 [M_1 \triangleright M_3 \wedge M_2 \triangleright M_3]]$$

If there are two diverging $\triangleright$-steps from some term and $\triangleright$ satisfies the diamond property, then there is always a way to converge again.

Definition 3.12 (Church–Rosser) *A notion of reduction R is said to be Church–Rosser (CR) if $\twoheadrightarrow_R \models \Diamond$.*

We then have the following theorem:

Theorem 3.13 (Church–Rosser Theorem)
Let R be CR, then:

$$M =_R N \Rightarrow \exists Z [M \twoheadrightarrow_R Z \wedge N \twoheadrightarrow_R Z]$$

Proof

By induction on the definition of $=_R$:

(i) $M =_R N$ because $M \twoheadrightarrow_R N$: Choose $Z \equiv N$

(ii) $M =_R N$ because $N =_R M$: trivial

(iii) $M =_R N$ because $M =_R L$ and $L =_R N$: by IH twice:

$$\exists Z_1 [M \twoheadrightarrow_R Z_1 \wedge L \twoheadrightarrow_R Z_1]$$

and

$$\exists Z_2[L \twoheadrightarrow_R Z_2 \wedge N \twoheadrightarrow_R Z_2]$$

and therefore, since:

$$L \twoheadrightarrow_R Z_1$$

and

$$L \twoheadrightarrow_R Z_2$$

together with the fact that R is CR, there is a Z such that:

$$Z_1 \twoheadrightarrow_R Z \qquad \text{and} \qquad Z_2 \twoheadrightarrow_R Z$$

and thus we have the desired result. □

This theorem has a useful corollary:

Corollary 3.3.1 *Let R be CR, then:*
(i) if N is an R-nf of M then $M \twoheadrightarrow_R N$
(ii) a term can have at most one R-nf

Proof
(i) Let $M =_R N$, where N is a R-nf. Then by the theorem there is a Z such that $M \twoheadrightarrow_R Z$ and $N \twoheadrightarrow_R Z$. But since N is an R-nf, we have $N \equiv Z$.
(ii) Let N_1 and N_2 both be R-nfs of M. Then $N_1 =_R M =_R N_2$ and so $N_1 =_R N_2$ and thus there is a Z to which both normal forms reduce (by the theorem); therefore

$$N_1 \equiv Z \equiv N_2$$

□

Thus if we can demonstrate that β is CR, we will have answered our first question. In fact the corollary tells us more; not only does it guarantee unicity of normal forms for terms, it also guarantees that if a term has a normal form then it will be possible to reduce the term to it.

To demonstrate that β is CR we must show $\twoheadrightarrow_\beta \models \diamond$. First some notation; if $\rhd$ is some binary relation on a set X then we write $\rhd^*$ for its transitive closure and we have:

$$\rhd \models \diamond \Rightarrow \rhd^* \models \diamond$$

which can be justified by consideration of the following diagram:

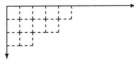

The axes represent diverging reductions, the side of each small square represents a single step. The small internal squares, (some of which are) shown with dashed lines, can all be completed by appealing to the CR property for ▷. So if we could show that the reflexive closure of one-step β-reduction satisfies the diamond property, we would have finished. Alas, life is never that simple! Consider the following term:

$$(\lambda x.xx)((\lambda x.x)(\lambda x.x))$$

Then we have the following pair of divergent reductions:

$$(\lambda x.xx)((\lambda x.x)(\lambda x.x)) \to_\beta ((\lambda x.x)(\lambda x.x))((\lambda x.x)(\lambda x.x))$$

$$(\lambda x.xx)((\lambda x.x)(\lambda x.x)) \to_\beta (\lambda x.xx)(\lambda x.x)$$

But while in the second case there is then only one redex:

$$(\lambda x.xx)(\lambda x.x) \to_\beta (\lambda x.x)(\lambda x.x)$$

there is no way of converging to this term by one step in the first case. So we cannot directly apply the above result to show that β is CR. The approach that we will take involves introducing a new relation which is "sandwiched" by the reflexive closure of $\to_\beta$ and $\twoheadrightarrow_\beta$ and which has $\twoheadrightarrow_\beta$ as its transitive closure.

We define the relation $\twoheadrightarrow_1$. This relation is reflexive and allows multiple β-reductions in one step. We read "$M \twoheadrightarrow_1 N$" as "M grand reduces to N". The intuition is that $\twoheadrightarrow_1$ can perform multiple $\to_\beta$ steps in one big step.

Definition 3.14 (Grand Reduction)
$\twoheadrightarrow_1$ *is defined in the following way:*

$$M \twoheadrightarrow_1 M$$

$$\frac{M \twoheadrightarrow_1 M'}{\lambda x.M \twoheadrightarrow_1 \lambda x.M'}$$

$$\frac{M \twoheadrightarrow_1 M' \quad N \twoheadrightarrow_1 N'}{MN \twoheadrightarrow_1 M'N'}$$

$$\frac{M \twoheadrightarrow_1 M' \quad N \twoheadrightarrow_1 N'}{(\lambda x.M)N \twoheadrightarrow_1 M'[x := N']}$$

Notice that, since $\twoheadrightarrow_1$ is reflexive, both of the divergent $\to_\beta$ steps are also $\twoheadrightarrow_1$ steps. There are two additional $\twoheadrightarrow_1$ steps, the first uses reflexivity and the second results in the term $(\lambda x.x)(\lambda x.x)$ (by using the fourth clause in the definition). Evidence that $\twoheadrightarrow_1$ is weaker than $\twoheadrightarrow_\beta$ is furnished by the fact that:

$$(\lambda x.xx)((\lambda x.x)(\lambda x.x)) \twoheadrightarrow_\beta \lambda x.x$$

but the corresponding grand reduction requires at least two steps.

Exercise 3.3.1
(i) Show that $\to_\beta$ is included in $\twoheadrightarrow_1$.
(ii) Write down the various $\twoheadrightarrow_1$ reduction sequences that start with the following term: $(\lambda x.xx)((\lambda x.x)(\lambda x.x))$

The following properties of $\twoheadrightarrow_1$ can all be proved by induction on the definition of the relation:

(1) $M \twoheadrightarrow_1 M', N \twoheadrightarrow_1 N' \Rightarrow M[x := N] \twoheadrightarrow_1 M'[x := N']$

(2) $\lambda x.M \twoheadrightarrow_1 N \Rightarrow N \equiv \lambda x.M'$ with $M \twoheadrightarrow_1 M'$

(3) $MN \twoheadrightarrow_1 L$ implies either:

  (a) $L \equiv M'N'$ with $M \twoheadrightarrow_1 M'$ and $N \twoheadrightarrow_1 N'$
  (b) or $M \equiv \lambda x.P, L \equiv P'[x := N']$ with $P \twoheadrightarrow_1 P'$ and $N \twoheadrightarrow_1 N'$

(4) $\twoheadrightarrow_1 \models \diamond$

We will show the second and fourth properties.

Lemma 3.15 $\lambda x.M \twoheadrightarrow_1 N \Rightarrow N \equiv \lambda x.M'$ *with* $M \twoheadrightarrow_1 M'$

Proof
$N \equiv \lambda x.M$: trivial

$N \equiv \lambda x.M'$ and $M \twoheadrightarrow_1 M'$: trivial

The other cases of the definition do not apply. $\square$

Lemma 3.16 $\twoheadrightarrow_1 \models \diamond$

Proof
The proof is by induction on the definition of $M \twoheadrightarrow_1 M_1$; we show that for all M_2 such that $M \twoheadrightarrow_1 M_2$, there is an M_3 such that $M_1 \twoheadrightarrow_1 M_3$ and $M_2 \twoheadrightarrow_1 M_3$.

$M_1 \equiv M$: choose $M_3 \equiv M_2$.

$M \equiv \lambda x.P$ and $M_1 \equiv \lambda x.P'$ and $P \twoheadrightarrow_1 P'$: By the previous lemma M_2 must be of the form $\lambda x.P''$ with $P \twoheadrightarrow_1 P''$. By IH P' and P'' have a common reduct, say P'''; we choose $M_3 \equiv \lambda x.P'''$.

$M \equiv PQ$, $M_1 \equiv P'Q'$ and $P \twoheadrightarrow_1 P'$, $Q \twoheadrightarrow_1 Q'$: from the properties listed above there are two cases to consider.

(i) $M_2 \equiv P''Q''$ with $P \twoheadrightarrow_1 P''$ and $Q \twoheadrightarrow_1 Q''$: then by the IH P' and P'' (respectively Q' and Q'') have a common reduct P''' (respectively Q''') and we can take $M_3 \equiv P'''Q'''$.

(ii) $M_2 \equiv P_1''[x := Q'']$ with $P \equiv \lambda x.P_1$, $P_1 \twoheadrightarrow_1 P_1''$ and $Q \twoheadrightarrow_1 Q''$: then by the previous lemma, $P' \equiv \lambda x.P_1'$ with $P_1 \twoheadrightarrow_1 P_1'$. By the IH applied to Q', Q'' and P_1', P_1'' there is a common reduct of M_1 and M_2 which is $P_1'''[x := Q''']$.

$M \equiv (\lambda x.P)Q$, $M_1 \equiv P'[x := Q']$ and $P \twoheadrightarrow_1 P'$, $Q \twoheadrightarrow_1 Q'$: again there are two cases depending on whether $M_2 \equiv P''[x := Q'']$ or $M_2 \equiv (\lambda x.P'')Q''$; in both cases the appropriate argumentation is similar to the previous case.

$\square$

Finally, we have the result that we have been waiting for:

Theorem 3.17 $\twoheadrightarrow_\beta$ *is the transitive closure of* $\twoheadrightarrow_1$

Proof
Sketch
From Exercise 3.3.1, it is easy to see that the reflexive closure of $\rightarrow_\beta$ is included in $\twoheadrightarrow_1$. It is also easy to see that $\twoheadrightarrow_\beta \supset \twoheadrightarrow_1$ and then, since $\twoheadrightarrow_\beta$ is the transitive closure of the reflexive closure of $\rightarrow_\beta$, it is also the transitive closure of $\twoheadrightarrow_1$. $\square$

From this result and property 4 of $\twoheadrightarrow_1$ we have that β is CR.

Therefore, using the corollary to the theorem that started this section, we know that β-nfs are unique and that, if a term has a β-nf then it is possible to reduce it to that nf. This allows us to prove the consistency of the theory λ. First, we need to prove the following:

Proposition 3.18 $M =_\beta N \Leftrightarrow \lambda \vdash M = N$

Proof
($\Rightarrow$): By induction on the definitions of the relations involved. (**Exercise**)
($\Leftarrow$): By induction on the length of the proof of $M = N$. (**Exercise**) $\square$

Consistency follows because:

$$M = N$$

is not a theorem for any two distinct normal forms (because by the Church–Rosser Theorem they would have to have a common contractum for the equality to hold).

We can also define a notion of reduction which is related to the extensional theory $\lambda\eta$:

$$\eta = \{(\lambda x.Mx, M) \mid x \notin FV(M)\}$$

We can define one-step η-reduction, η-reduction and η-convertibility in the standard way. It is then possible to address the question "Is η CR?"; however, a more interesting question is whether the derived notion $\beta\eta$ (=

$\beta \cup \eta)$ is. It turns out that both η and $\beta\eta$ are CR and the interested reader is referred to Barendregt for more detail.

Newman's Lemma

An alternative strategy for proving that a notion of reduction is CR uses Newman's Lemma. First we make a few more definitions:

Definition 3.19 *A binary relation,* $\triangleright$*, on a set* X *satisfies the* weak diamond property *if:*

$$\forall M, M_1, M_2[M \triangleright M_1 \wedge M \triangleright M_2 \Rightarrow \exists M_3[M_1 \triangleright^*_{\underline{\ }} M_3 \wedge M_2 \triangleright^*_{\underline{\ }} M_3]]$$

where $\triangleright^*_{\underline{\ }}$ *is the reflexive, transitive closure of* $\triangleright$*.*

Compare this to the diamond property; here the reductions diverge in one step but there may be many (or zero) steps for them to re-converge. The converging reduction sequences need not have the same number of steps. The reduction relation $\rightarrow_\beta$ does satisfy the weak diamond property.

Definition 3.20 R *is* Weakly Church–Rosser (WCR) *if* $\rightarrow_R$ *satisfies the weak diamond property.*

Definition 3.21 *For* $M \in \Lambda$*:*

(1) M R-strongly normalises $(R\text{-}SN(M))$ *if there is no infinite R-reduction starting with M.*

(2) M *is* R-infinite $(R\text{-}\infty(M))$ *if not $R\text{-}SN(M)$.*

(3) R *is* Strongly Normalising (SN) *if:*

$$\forall M \in \Lambda.R\text{-}SN(M)$$

Examples of (1) for β are:

$$\lambda x.x \text{ and } (\lambda x.xx)((\lambda x.x)(\lambda x.x))$$

But:

$$\beta\text{-}\infty((\lambda x.xx)(\lambda x.xx)) \text{ and } \beta\text{-}\infty((\lambda x.y)((\lambda x.xx)(\lambda x.xx)))$$

The second example is instructive since it shows that terms can be β-infinite but have normal forms. Because of the existence of these latter examples, it is clear that β is not SN and thus the following is not applicable (however it will be useful for the simple typed λ-calculus). Newman's Lemma is stated as follows:

Lemma 3.22 (Newman's Lemma)

$$SN \wedge WCR \Rightarrow CR$$

The proof of this lemma uses the notion of *ambiguity*: we say that a term is ambiguous if it R-reduces to two distinct R-nfs. To show CR, it is sufficient to show that every term has a unique normal form, because of the SN property.

Proof [of Newman's Lemma]
By SN every term R-reduces to an R-nf. Suppose a term M is ambiguous, i.e. $M\twoheadrightarrow_R M_1$ and $M\twoheadrightarrow_R M_2$ with M_1, M_2 distinct R-nfs. Now consider M' such that $M \to_R M'$, there are two cases:

(i) $M \to_R M'\twoheadrightarrow_R M_1$: then there is also a term M'' such that $M \to_R M''\twoheadrightarrow_R M_2$ and by WCR there is a term M''' such that $M'\twoheadrightarrow_R M'''$ and $M''\twoheadrightarrow_R M'''$. From our initial observation, there is a normal form M_3 to which M''' reduces and thus $M'\twoheadrightarrow_R M_1$ and $M'\twoheadrightarrow_R M_3$.

(ii) there is no divergent reduction from M: in this case the ambiguity of M arises from a divergence after the initial reduction $M \to_R M'$.

In either case we have that for every ambiguous term M, there is another ambiguous term M' such that $M \to_R M'$. This situation is prohibited by SN – therefore there are no ambiguous terms, i.e. every term has a unique normal form.

$\square$

Thus the alternative strategy involves showing SN and WCR separately and then inferring CR.

Reduction Graphs

We close this section by introducing the notion of reduction graphs; a useful pedagogical tool:

Definition 3.23 *The R-reduction graph of a term M, written $G_R(M)$, is the set:*

$$\{N \in \Lambda \mid M\twoheadrightarrow_R N\}$$

directed by $\to_R$.

If several redexes give rise to $M_0 \to_R M_1$, then that many directed arcs connect M_0 to M_1.

Example 3.24 $G_\beta(WWW)$ *with* $W \equiv \lambda xy.xyy$ *is:*

$$
\begin{array}{ccc}
WWW & \longleftarrow & (\lambda y.yyy)W \\
\uparrow\downarrow & & \uparrow \\
(\lambda y.Wyy)W & \longrightarrow\!\!\!\!\!\longleftarrow & (\lambda y.(\lambda z.yzz)y)W
\end{array}
$$

and $G_\beta((\lambda x.xx)(\lambda x.xx))$ *is:*

$$(\lambda x.xx)(\lambda x.xx)$$

Notice that the fact that M has a β-nf does not imply that $G_\beta(M)$ is finite; just consider the term:

$$M \equiv (\lambda xy.y)(\omega_3\omega_3) \text{ with } \omega_3 \equiv \lambda x.xxx$$

then M has β-nf $\lambda y.y$ but:

Exercise 3.3.2 *Draw $G_\beta(M)$.*

Neither does the fact that $G_\beta(M)$ is finite imply that M has a β-nf; just consider the second graph above. However, we do have the following result, which relates graphs and the notion of strong normalisation:

Proposition 3.25 β-$SN(M) \Rightarrow G_\beta(M)$ *is finite and M has a β-nf.*

Proof Since we are dealing with finite terms, each term contains a finite number of redexes and thus the reduction graph is finitely branching. Since we have β-$SN(M)$, we have that there are no infinite paths through $G_\beta(M)$. Thus, by König's Lemma, $G_\beta(M)$ is finite. Moreover the absence of infinite paths implies that the graph is acyclic; thus there must be a terminal node, the β-nf of M. □

However the converse does not hold; just consider

$$G_\beta((\lambda xy.y)((\lambda x.xx)(\lambda x.xx)))$$

3.4   Delta Rules

The pure, type free λ-calculus is an extremely powerful formalism. Indeed, all computable functions are representable as λ-terms as we shall see later. Such representations use clever coding tricks. For example a possible coding of integers is equivalent to using the data type specification:

$$num = Zero \mid Succ\ num$$

so that 5 (say) is represented as $Succ(Succ(Succ(Succ(Succ\ Zero))))$ and the arithmetic operations are coded up as recursive functions, for example:

$$
\begin{aligned}
plus(m, Zero) &= m \\
plus(m, Succ(n)) &= plus(Succ(m), n)
\end{aligned}
$$

An alternative to this approach is to add constants to the notation along with associated reduction rules (so-called δ-rules).

If δ is some constant, we write $\Lambda\delta$ to represent the class of terms constructed from the usual alphabet plus δ. A δ-rule is then of the form[3]:

$$\delta\vec{M} \to E(\vec{M})$$

An example, introduced by Church, is:

$$\delta_C MN \to \lambda xy.x \text{ if } M, N \in \beta\delta_C\text{-}nf^0, M \equiv N$$
$$\delta_C MN \to \lambda xy.y \text{ if } M, N \in \beta\delta_C\text{-}nf^0, M \not\equiv N$$

where $\beta\delta_C\text{-}nf^0$ are closed $\beta\delta_C$ normal forms.

Several remarks are in order. First, as we shall see later, $\lambda xy.x$ is a standard encoding for *true* and $\lambda xy.y$ is a standard encoding for *false*. Thus δ_C is effectively a predicate which determines if two closed $\beta\delta_C$ normal forms are equivalent. It is important that the δ-rules should specify closed terms to avoid inconsistency:

$$(\lambda xy.\delta_C xy)\mathbf{II} \twoheadrightarrow \delta_C\mathbf{II} \to \lambda xy.x$$

but if δ_C can be applied to open terms then we also have:

$$(\lambda xy.\delta_C xy)\mathbf{II} \to (\lambda xyzw.w)\mathbf{II} \twoheadrightarrow \lambda zw.w$$

Now,

$$\lambda xy.x = \lambda zw.w$$
$$\Rightarrow (\lambda xy.x)MN = (\lambda zw.w)MN$$
$$\Rightarrow M = N$$

for arbitrary M, N. For reasons that we will return to below, it is also important that δ_C operates on normal forms.

However, caution is required. Even quite innocuous looking rules can disturb the Church–Rosser property. This is illustrated by the following example. We consider $\Lambda cons, head, tail$ with the rules (collectively called *SP* for "surjective pairing"):

$$head(consM_1M_2) \quad \to M_1$$
$$tail(consM_1M_2) \quad \to M_2$$
$$cons(headM)(tailM) \to M$$

Klop shows that βSP is not CR. We will content ourselves with an informal treatment of the proof since it requires some new theory which is beyond the scope of the current work. The problem can be illustrated in a simpler theory involving constants δ and ϵ and the rule:

$$\delta MM \to \epsilon$$

We can define λ-terms which have the following properties:

---

[3]We use the notation $E(M)$ to denote some arbitrary expression involving M.

$$Cx \twoheadrightarrow \delta x (Cx)$$

$$A \twoheadrightarrow CA$$

Both terms make use of fixed point combinators but not the particular one that we have used in the foregoing. The reader is encouraged to return to this point after reading Chapter 6. Then:

$$A \twoheadrightarrow CA \twoheadrightarrow \delta A(CA) \twoheadrightarrow \delta(CA)(CA) \to \epsilon$$

but also:

$$A \twoheadrightarrow CA \twoheadrightarrow C(CA) \twoheadrightarrow C(\delta A(CA)) \twoheadrightarrow C(\delta(CA)(CA)) \to C\epsilon$$

and now it can be shown there is no reduction sequence from $C\epsilon$ which results in ϵ.

So how can we be sure that we will not disturb the CR property? Fortunately, there is a theorem, due to Mitschke, which gives conditions under which CR is preserved and we now present this. We start by defining what it means for two binary relations to commute:

Definition 3.26 Let $\triangleright_1$ and $\triangleright_2$ be binary relations on X. $\triangleright_1$ and $\triangleright_2$ commute *if:*

$$\forall x, x_1, x_2 \in X[x \triangleright_1 x_1 \wedge x \triangleright_2 x_2 \Rightarrow \exists x_3 \in X[x_1 \triangleright_2 x_3 \wedge x_2 \triangleright_1 x_3]]$$

Notice that $\triangleright \models \diamond$ if and only if $\triangleright$ commutes with itself (which follows from the definition). An important (useful) lemma which makes use of this notion of commutativity is due to Hindley and Rosen:

Lemma 3.27 (Hindley–Rosen Lemma)
(i) Let $\triangleright_1$ and $\triangleright_2$ be binary relations on X. Suppose
  (1) $\triangleright_1 \models \diamond$ and $\triangleright_2 \models \diamond$
  (2) $\triangleright_1$ commutes with $\triangleright_2$
then $(\triangleright_1 \cup \triangleright_2)^* \models \diamond$ (where $(\triangleright_1 \cup \triangleright_2)^*$ is the transitive closure of the combined relation).
(ii) Let R_1 and R_2 be two notions of reduction. Suppose
  (1) R_1 and R_2 are CR
  (2)$\twoheadrightarrow_{R_1}$ commutes with $\twoheadrightarrow_{R_2}$
then $R_1 \cup R_2$ is CR.

Proof
(i) Consider the following diagram:

the numbers indicate which relation is used in the step. All of the dotted squares can be filled appealing to either (1) or (2).

(ii) Follows from (i), since $\twoheadrightarrow_{R_1 R_2}$ is $(\twoheadrightarrow_{R_1} \cup \twoheadrightarrow_{R_2})^*$ □

We can now state Mitschke's theorem:

Theorem 3.28 *Let δ be some constant. Let $R_1, \ldots, R_m$ be n-ary relations on $\Lambda\delta$ and let $N_1, \ldots, N_m$ be arbitrary terms in $\Lambda\delta$. Introduce the notion of reduction δ by the following rules:*

$$\delta\vec{M} \to N_1 \ \text{if } R_1(\vec{M})$$
$$\cdots$$
$$\delta\vec{M} \to N_m \ \text{if } R_m(\vec{M})$$

Call this collection of rules δ_M. Then $\beta\delta_M$ is CR provided that:
(1) The R_i are disjoint
(2) The R_i are closed under $\beta\delta_M$-reduction and substitution, that is:
   $R_i(\vec{M}) \Rightarrow R_i(\vec{M'})$ *if* $\vec{M}\twoheadrightarrow_{\beta\delta_M} \vec{M'}$ *or* $\vec{M'}$ *is a substitution instance of* $\vec{M}$.

Not surprisingly, the proof of this theorem is quite complex! We will present a sketch of the main steps:

Proof
Sketch:

Step 1
Show that δ_M is CR by showing that the reflexive closure of $\to_{\delta_M} \models \diamond$; this is a straightforward case analysis (2 cases: disjoint redexes and overlapping redexes) which uses the fact that the R_i are closed under δ_M-reduction.

Step 2
Show that β and δ_M commute by considering the relative positions of the β and δ_M redexes. For example, suppose we perform a β-step first, then:
(1) if the β-redex is inside the δ_M-redex then, since the R_i are closed under β-reduction, the δ_M-redex is preserved.
(2) if the δ_M-redex is in the body of the function subterm of the β-redex then, since the R_i are closed under substitution, the δ_M-redex is preserved.

(3) if the δ_M-redex is a subterm of the argument in the β-redex then it may be duplicated.

(4) if the redexes are disjoint then the δ_M-redex is trivially preserved. Similar considerations for doing the δ_M-redex first give:

$$\forall M, M_1, M_2[M \rightarrow_\beta M_1 \wedge M \rightarrow_{\delta_M} M_2 \Rightarrow \exists M_3[M_1 \twoheadrightarrow_{\delta_M} M_3 \wedge M_2 \twoheadrightarrow_\beta M_3]]$$

and then commutativity of $\twoheadrightarrow_\beta$ and $\twoheadrightarrow_{\delta_M}$ follows by a diagram chase.

Step 3

Thus $\beta\delta_M$ is CR by the lemma of Hindley–Rosen (ii) $\square$

Exercise 3.4.1 *Complete this proof.*

So how does the rule:

$$\delta M M \rightarrow \epsilon$$

fall foul of the requirements of Mitschke's theorem? First, notice that we should more correctly write the rule in the following way:

$$\delta M N \rightarrow \epsilon \text{ if } M \equiv N$$

Now the predicate is not closed under $\beta\delta$-reduction; we can do different amounts of reduction to the two arguments and lose syntactic equality. As a final note, Church's rules do pass the test because of the insistence that M and N are $\beta\delta_C$ normal forms.

3.5   Residuals

In the following we will often want to trace a redex through a reduction sequence. Of course the redex, or more generally subterm, may be transformed through the sequence. For example, in the following (contrived) sequence:

$$\begin{aligned} &(\lambda xy.(\lambda zw.xz)y)MN \\ \rightarrow_\beta\ &(\underline{\lambda y.(\lambda zw.Mz)y})N \\ \rightarrow_\beta\ &(\lambda zw.Mz)N \\ \rightarrow_\beta\ &\lambda w.MN \end{aligned}$$

the underlined redexes are clearly related though different; notice that there is no remnant of the redex in the final term (it was reduced in the preceding line). We formalise this by introducing the notion of *descendants* of a subterm; we reserve the name *residual* for the descendant of a redex. We follow Klop and Lévy by introducing these notions via a labelled variant of the λ-calculus.

Terms in the labelled λ-calculus are words over the usual alphabet plus a label set, $\mathcal{A}$ (for example $\mathcal{A}$ might be $\mathcal{Z}_{\geq 0}$ - the positive integers):

Definition 3.29
$\Lambda_{\mathcal{A}}$ *is the set of labelled λ-terms defined inductively by:*

(1) $x^a \in \Lambda_{\mathcal{A}}, a \in \mathcal{A}$, x *a variable*
(2) *If* $M \in \Lambda_{\mathcal{A}}$ *and* $a \in \mathcal{A}$ *then* $(\lambda x.M)^a \in \Lambda_{\mathcal{A}}$
(3) *If* $M, N \in \Lambda_{\mathcal{A}}$ *and* $a \in \mathcal{A}$ *then* $(MN)^a \in \Lambda_{\mathcal{A}}$

For example:

$$((\lambda x.(x^1 x^2)^3)^4 (y^5 z^6)^7)^8$$

We can develop a theory for this calculus which closely mirrors λ; rather than do that we will just define the rule (β) and associated substitution operation and leave the reader to fill in the remaining details. Since we can view labels as colours which are attached to terms and which have no effect on computation (but are preserved by reduction) the theory is similar to our earlier development. The new rule (β) is:

$$((\lambda x.A)^a B)^b = A[x := B]$$

Notice that A and B are labelled terms and their labels are preserved but the labels a and b disappear. This is reasonable since a labels the function part of the redex and b labels the redex; neither of these plays any further rôle in the reduction sequence once the redex has been reduced. The substitution operation has to respect labels:

Definition 3.30
$$
\begin{aligned}
x^a[x := B] &\equiv B \\
y^a[x := B] &\equiv y^a, y \text{ distinct from } x \\
(MN)^a[x := B] &\equiv (M[x := B]N[x := B])^a \\
(\lambda y.M)^a[x := B] &\equiv (\lambda y.M[x := B])^a
\end{aligned}
$$

For example, corresponding to the unlabelled term:

$$(((\lambda x.(\lambda y.y))((\lambda x.xx)(\lambda x.xx)))((\lambda x.x)z))$$

we have the following labelled term and reduction sequence:

$$
\begin{aligned}
&(((\lambda x.(\lambda y.y^1)^2)^3((\lambda x.x^4 x^5)^6(\lambda x.x^7 x^8)^9)^{10})^{11}((\lambda x.x^{12})^{13} z^{14})^{15})^{16} \\
&\to_\beta ((\lambda y.y^1)^2((\lambda x.x^{12})^{13} z^{14})^{15})^{16} \\
&\to_\beta ((\lambda x.x^{12})^{13} z^{14})^{15} \\
&\to_\beta z^{14}
\end{aligned}
$$

Definition 3.31 *Let M be an unlabelled λ-term and $\mathcal{A}$ a label set. A labelling is a function, $\mathcal{I}$, mapping each subterm to a label. We call a labelling initial if it labels distinct subterms with distinct labels.*

For a reduction Δ, we have the labelled equivalent, Δ^*:

$$\Delta^* : \mathcal{I}(M) \to^\Delta \mathcal{J}(N) \text{ for some labellings } \mathcal{I} \text{ and } \mathcal{J}$$

where we have used the superscript on the reduction arrow to indicate the
redex that is being reduced.

Definition 3.32 *If $\mathcal{I}(S) = \mathcal{J}(T)$ for $S \in Sub(M)$ and $T \in Sub(N)$ then
T is a* descendant *of S. As already mentioned, the descendant of a redex
is called a* residual *and the redex that we contract at each stage has no
residuals.*

3.6 Head Normal Forms

We now introduce an alternative form of normal form: *head normal form.*
Head normal forms play an important rôle in the theory and they are much
closer to the concept of "answer" employed in lazy functional programming
languages, as we shall see.

We start with some formal definitions:

Definition 3.33 *$M \in \Lambda$ is a* head normal form (hnf) *if M is of the form:*

$$\lambda x_1 \ldots x_n.x M_1 \ldots M_m \qquad n, m \geq 0$$

In this case x is called the head variable.
*If $M \equiv \lambda x_1 \ldots x_n.(\lambda x.M_0)M_1 \ldots M_m$ where $n \geq 0, m \geq 1$ then the subterm
$(\lambda x.M_0)M_1$ is called the* head redex *of M.*

Some examples of head normal forms are:

- xM
- $\lambda x.x$
- $\lambda xy.x$
- $\lambda xy.x((\lambda z.z)y)$
- $\lambda y.z$

If

$$M \to^\Delta N$$

and Δ is the head redex of M, then we write:

$$M \to_h N$$

and we also write $\twoheadrightarrow_h$ for the many-step reduction relation.

Definition 3.34 *If A and B are two redexes in an expression M and the
first occurrence of λ in A is to the left of the first occurrence of λ in B then
we say that A is* to the left *of B. If A is a redex in M and it is to the left
of all of the other redexes then A is the* leftmost *redex.*

Notice that the head redex of a term is always the leftmost but not con-
versely; consider:

$$\lambda xy.x((\lambda z.z)y)$$

this term is an hnf (i.e. it has no head redex!) and so the leftmost redex is the *internal redex*:

$$(\lambda z.z)y$$

(**Note**: a redex is internal if it is not a head redex).

Unlike normal forms, a term does not usually have a unique head normal form. For example:

$$(\lambda x.x(\mathbf{II}))z \text{ where } \mathbf{I} \equiv \lambda x.x$$

has hnf's

- $z(\mathbf{II})$
- and $z\mathbf{I}$

However, since any term has only one head redex, every term which has an hnf has a *principal head normal form* which is reached by reducing the head redex at each stage until the head normal form is reached. The principal head normal form of the example is $z(\mathbf{II})$.

Head normal forms play a crucial rôle in the Computability Theory associated with the λ-calculus. There must be some way of coding partial functions — functions which are undefined for some elements in the domain. Readers familiar with denotational semantics will have already met this problem; in domain theory, partial functions are made into total functions by adding an undefined element $\perp$ (pronounced "bottom") to the co-domain. In the λ-calculus, the solution is to use a class of terms to represent the undefined element. The first attempt at solving this problem involved equating all of the terms without normal form and then using some canonical representative as the undefined element. However, this leads to inconsistency because neither:

$$\lambda x.x\mathbf{K}\Omega \text{ where } \mathbf{K} \equiv \lambda xy.x \text{ and } \Omega \equiv (\lambda x.xx)(\lambda x.xx)$$

nor:

$$\lambda x.x\mathbf{S}\Omega \text{ where } \mathbf{S} \equiv \lambda xyz.xz(yz)$$

has an nf but it is easy to show that $\lambda+(\lambda x.x\mathbf{K}\Omega = \lambda x.x\mathbf{S}\Omega)$ is inconsistent:

$$\lambda x.x\mathbf{K}\Omega = \lambda x.x\mathbf{S}\Omega \Rightarrow (\lambda x.x\mathbf{K}\Omega)\mathbf{K} = (\lambda x.x\mathbf{S}\Omega)\mathbf{K}$$
$$\Rightarrow \mathbf{KK}\Omega = \mathbf{KS}\Omega$$
$$\Rightarrow \mathbf{K} = \mathbf{S}$$

but we saw in Chapter 2 that $\mathbf{K}\#\mathbf{S}$. Instead, we equate all terms which do not have a head normal form (this is a proper sub-class of the class of terms without nf); this leads to no inconsistency, a canonical representative is Ω.

Practical lazy functional programming systems even stop some way short of hnf. Most lazy systems evaluate terms to *weak head normal form*. A weak head normal form is a term of the form:

$$xM_0 \ldots M_n \text{ where } n \geq 0$$

or

$$\lambda x.M$$

that is, lazy systems do not evaluate inside λs. We will return to this issue later when we consider the Lazy λ-calculus.

3.7   The Standardisation Theorem

Definition 3.35 *A reduction sequence:*

$$\sigma : M_0 \to^{\Delta_0} M_1 \to^{\Delta_1} M_2 \to^{\Delta_2} \ldots$$

is a standard reduction *if* $\forall i.\forall j < i.\Delta_i$ *is not a residual of a redex to the left of* Δ_j *relative to the given reduction from* M_j *to* M_i.

An alternative description of a standard reduction is as follows: after reduction of each redex R, all of the λs to the left of R are marked indelibly; no redex whose first λ is marked can be further reduced.

If there is a standard reduction from some term M to some other term N then we write $M \twoheadrightarrow_s N$. Notice that any head reduction sequence is a standard reduction sequence.

We have already defined an internal redex to be any redex which is not a head redex. We write:

$$M \twoheadrightarrow_i N$$

if there is a reduction sequence:

$$M \equiv M_0 \to^{\Delta_0} M_1 \to^{\Delta_1} \ldots \to^{\Delta_{n-1}} M_n \equiv N$$

such that each of the Δ_i is an internal reduction in M_i. Before we can prove the Standardisation Theorem, we must state a result which allows us to factor reductions into a sequence of head reductions followed by a sequence of internal reductions. The proof of the following result can be found in Barendregt's book.

Proposition 3.36 $M \twoheadrightarrow N \Rightarrow \exists Z[M \twoheadrightarrow_h Z \twoheadrightarrow_i N]$

The details of the proof use some additional theory which is beyond the scope of this book; it relies on two observations:

- If $M \to_i M' \twoheadrightarrow_h N'$, then there is an equivalent reduction sequence $M \twoheadrightarrow_h N \twoheadrightarrow_i N'$.

- Any reduction sequence $M \twoheadrightarrow N$ is of the form

$$M \twoheadrightarrow_h M_1 \twoheadrightarrow_i M_2 \twoheadrightarrow_h M_3 \twoheadrightarrow_i \ldots \twoheadrightarrow_i N$$

The intuition behind the first observation is the difference between call-by-value and call-by-name: an internal redex is an argument, so if we pre-evaluate it we only need do it once, if we don't pre-evaluate it then it may be duplicated. Since any reduction is either a head reduction or an internal reduction, the second observation is straightforward.

We then have the Standardisation Theorem:

Theorem 3.37 (The Standardisation Theorem)

$$M \twoheadrightarrow N \Rightarrow M \twoheadrightarrow_s N$$

Proof
We prove this result by induction on $\| N \|$, the number of symbols in N. By the previous result, we have:

$$\exists Z [M \twoheadrightarrow_h Z \twoheadrightarrow_i N]$$

and there are two cases to consider:

Case 1
N is a variable, say x. Then $Z \equiv x$ and so $M \twoheadrightarrow_h N$ and since a head reduction is standard, we are done.

Case 2
$N \equiv \lambda x_0 \ldots x_n . N_0 N_1 \ldots N_m$ with $n + m > 0$
Then Z must be of the form $\lambda x_0 \ldots x_n . Z_0 \ldots Z_m$ with $Z_i \twoheadrightarrow N_i$ for $0 \leq i \leq m$.
By the IH $Z_i \twoheadrightarrow_s N_i$ and the result follows.   □

Thus we are able to answer the second question posed in the Introduction: since we know from the Corollary to the Church–Rosser Theorem that if M has a normal form N then $M \twoheadrightarrow N$, then by the Standardisation Theorem we know that a standard reduction sequence will lead to the normal form.

3.8 Summary

In this chapter we have studied various aspects of reduction. We have seen how this concept is related to the usual notion of evaluation used in functional languages. The two key results are the Church–Rosser theorem for β reduction, which guarantees determinacy of the evaluation process, and the Standardisation Theorem which identifies a canonical evaluation order for the reduction process. We have also seen how to extend the calculus with constants.

4

Combinatory Logic

Overview

The λ-calculus was invented in a historical period which was very active for Mathematical Logic. Inspired by Hilbert, many mathematicians were trying to capture the notion of effective calculability. Within the space of ten years the λ-calculus, Recursive Function Theory and Turing Machines were all invented. This chapter presents an equally important calculus from that era: Combinatory Logic. We start by introducing the notation and basic theory. All of the theory that we have developed for the λ-calculus could be recast for Combinatory Logic. Rather than do that we briefly summarise the key results. In the second section we consider the relationship between Combinatory Logic and the λ-calculus in more detail. The final topic in this chapter concerns the notion of a *basis*: the identification of a set of (λ-)terms from which all of the terms can be generated using only application.

4.1 Combinatory Logic

One of the fundamental properties of the λ-calculus is combinatory completeness:

Proposition 4.1 *Given an arbitrary λ-term containing some free variables, denoted by $M(\vec{x})$[1], it is possible to construct a new term F with the property that:*

$$F\vec{x} = M(\vec{x})$$

This property is called combinatory completeness. *There is an obvious candidate for F, i.e.:*

$$\lambda\vec{x}.M$$

However, a more remarkable result is that such an F can be constructed using the two combinators **S** and **K** and application (i.e. there is no need for abstraction). The theory which develops this latter approach is *Combinatory Logic*.

---

[1] This notation should be read as $FV(M)$ is a subset of $\vec{x}$.

Combinatory Logic was invented by Schönfinkel in 1924 and independently by Curry in 1930. The notation that we use in our presentation of the theory of combinators is due to Curry. The theory of combinators predates the earliest work on the λ-calculus which was introduced by Church in 1932. Our emphasis on the λ-calculus has been motivated by the fact that the λ-notation is a "higher-level" notation than combinators; combinatory terms look like assembly language programs! This last observation is reflected in the use that Computer Science has made of the two theories: the λ-calculus is often described as the canonical functional programming language but, while no high-level languages employ a notation based on the (low-level/fine grain) combinators of Combinatory Logic, many of the most successful implementations are based on combinator reduction. From a language implementation point of view, one of the attractions of combinator terms is that there are no bound variables and, consequently, the role of the environment (cf. Chapter 8) is diminished: this has important implications for distributed implementations in which access to an environment can be a major bottleneck.

The class of combinator terms is defined as follows:

Definition 4.2 *The class of CL-terms are words over the alphabet:*

$$x, y, z, \ldots \qquad variables$$
$$\mathbf{S}, \mathbf{K} \qquad constants$$
$$(,) \qquad parentheses$$

The class $\mathcal{C}$ of CL-terms is the least class satisfying the following:

(1) $x \in \mathcal{C}, x$ *a variable*

(2) $\mathbf{S} \in \mathcal{C}$

(3) $\mathbf{K} \in \mathcal{C}$

(4) *if $A, B \in \mathcal{C}$ then $(AB) \in \mathcal{C}$*

Thus example terms in $\mathcal{C}$ are:

$$\textbf{(SK)} \qquad \textbf{SKK} \qquad \textbf{S(KS)K}$$

Notice that adopting the convention that application is left associative allows us to omit some parentheses in the second two examples. All variables appearing in a CL-term are free; consequently:

$$P[x := Q]$$

denotes the substitution of Q for all occurrences of x in P. P is *closed* if and only if $FV(P) = \emptyset$; $\mathcal{C}^0 (= \{P \in \mathcal{C} \mid P \text{ closed}\})$ is the set of closed terms.

CL-formulae are of the form:

$$P = Q \text{ with } P, Q \in \mathcal{C}$$

The theory is defined by the following axioms and rules:

$$\mathbf{K}PQ = P$$

$$\mathbf{S}PQR = PR(QR)$$

$$P = P$$

$$\frac{P = Q}{Q = P}$$

$$\frac{P = Q \quad Q = R}{P = R}$$

$$\frac{P = P'}{PR = P'R}$$

$$\frac{P = P'}{RP = RP'}$$

Lemma 4.3 $CL \vdash \mathbf{SKK}A = A$

Proof
$\mathbf{SKK}A = \mathbf{K}A(\mathbf{K}A) = A$
The result follows by the transitivity of $=$. $\square$

   Motivated by this result, we define $\mathbf{I} \equiv \mathbf{SKK}$, then $\mathbf{I}$ is the identity combinator. Notice that this choice of definition for $\mathbf{I}$ is slightly arbitrary, since we have the following:

Lemma 4.4 $\forall M, N \in C.CL \vdash (\mathbf{SK}M)N = N$

Proof

$$\mathbf{SK}MN = \mathbf{K}N(MN)$$
$$= N$$

                                                                   $\square$

Exercise 4.1.1
1. Define $\mathbf{B} \equiv \mathbf{S(KS)K}$. Show that $CL \vdash \mathbf{B}MNP = M(NP)$. *[$\mathbf{B}$ is the composition operator.]*
2. Define $\mathbf{C} \equiv \mathbf{S(BS(BKS))(KK)}$. Show that $CL \vdash \mathbf{C}MNP = MPN$.

   Using these new combinators, we can state and prove a Fixed Point Theorem for Combinatory Logic:

Theorem 4.5 (The Fixed Point Theorem)

$$\forall F \in C.\exists X \in C.FX = X$$

Proof
Let $W \equiv \mathbf{B}F(\mathbf{SII})$ and $X \equiv WW$.
Then:

$$
\begin{aligned}
X &\equiv WW \\
&\equiv \mathbf{B}F(\mathbf{SII})W \\
&= F(\mathbf{SII}W) \\
&= F(IW(IW)) \\
&= F(WW) \\
&\equiv FX
\end{aligned}
$$

$\square$

We have seen how the definition of the fixed point combinator $\mathbf{Y}$ can be derived from the proof of the Fixed Point Theorem in λ; the corresponding CL-term is:

$$\mathbf{Y} \equiv \mathbf{S}(\mathbf{CB}(\mathbf{SII}))(\mathbf{CB}(\mathbf{SII}))$$

Exercise 4.1.2 *Verify that the CL-term $\mathbf{Y}$ is a fixed point combinator, i.e. $\mathbf{Y}F = F(\mathbf{Y}F)$.*

The definitions of $\mathbf{B}$, $\mathbf{C}$, $\mathbf{I}$ and $\mathbf{Y}$ seem to work but how did the author (or someone else!) decide that they were the appropriate definitions to use? We will return to this question in the next section, where we will study the relationship between the λ-calculus and Combinatory Logic. In preparation for this, we introduce a pseudo λ-abstraction operator, λ^*:

$$
\begin{aligned}
\lambda^*x.x &\equiv \mathbf{I} \\
\lambda^*x.P &\equiv \mathbf{K}P, \text{ if } x \notin FV(P) \\
\lambda^*x.PQ &\equiv \mathbf{S}(\lambda^*x.P)(\lambda^*x.Q)
\end{aligned}
$$

In the following we will abuse notation and write $\lambda^*xyz\ldots.$ for:

$$\lambda^*x.(\lambda^*y.(\lambda^*z.\ldots.))$$

It is possible to demonstrate that this is a good definition of abstraction; we do this by presenting some of the properties of λ^*:

Lemma 4.6

$$FV(\lambda^*x.P) = FV(P) - \{x\}$$

So the abstraction operator removes free variables; notice that it does not bind occurrences of x in quite the same way as λ, since x will not occur at all in $\lambda^*x.P$.

Proof
(induction on the structure of P)
$P \equiv x$: $FV(\lambda^*x.x) = FV(\mathbf{I}) = \emptyset = FV(x) - \{x\}$

$x \notin FV(P)$: $FV(\lambda^*x.P) = FV(\mathbf{K}P) = FV(P)$

$P \equiv MN$:

$$FV(\lambda^*x.MN) = FV(\mathbf{S}(\lambda^*x.M)(\lambda^*x.N))$$
$$= (FV(M) - \{x\}) \cup (FV(N) - \{x\})$$
$$= FV(P) - \{x\}$$

$\square$

Lemma 4.7

$$CL \vdash (\lambda^*x.P)x = P$$

Abstracting a variable and then applying the abstraction to the variable is convertible with the original term.

Proof
(induction on the structure of P) $\square$

Exercise 4.1.3 *Complete this proof*

Lemma 4.8

$$CL \vdash (\lambda^*x.P)Q = P[x := Q]$$

Compare with the β-conversion axiom of λ.

Proof
(induction on the structure of P)
$P \equiv x$: $(\lambda^*x.x)Q \equiv \mathbf{I}Q = Q \equiv P[x := Q]$

$x \notin FV(P)$: $(\lambda^*x.P)Q \equiv \mathbf{K}PQ = P \equiv P[x := Q]$

$P \equiv MN$:

$$(\lambda^*x.MN)Q \equiv \mathbf{S}(\lambda^*x.M)(\lambda^*x.N)Q$$
$$= (\lambda^*x.M)Q((\lambda^*x.N)Q)$$
$$= M[x := Q]N[x := Q] \text{ by IH twice}$$
$$\equiv P[x := Q]$$

(An alternative proof of this result may be found in Barendregt) $\square$

Lemma 4.9 *If x is distinct from y then $(\lambda^*x.P)[y := Q] = \lambda^*x.P[y := Q]$.*

Proof   (induction on the structure of P) $\square$

Exercise 4.1.4 *Complete this proof*

The condition that x and y be distinct in Lemma 4.9 is essential:

$$(\lambda^*xy.x)yQ \neq x[x := y][y := Q]$$

This motivates the adoption of a variable convention for CL. The convention is basically the same as that used for the λ-calculus but, while we had to work with equivalence classes of α-congruent terms there, here α-congruent terms are identical:

Lemma 4.10 *If $y \notin FV(P)$ then $\lambda^* x.P \equiv \lambda^* y.P[x := y]$*

Proof

(induction on the structure of P)

$P \equiv x$: $\lambda^* x.x \equiv \mathbf{I} \equiv \lambda^* y.x[x := y]$

$x \notin FV(P)$: $\lambda^* x.P \equiv \mathbf{K}P \equiv \lambda^* y.P \equiv \lambda^* y.P[x := y]$

$P \equiv MN$:

$$\begin{aligned}(\lambda^* x.MN) &\equiv \mathbf{S}(\lambda^* x.M)(\lambda^* x.N)\\ &\equiv \mathbf{S}(\lambda^* y.M[x := y])(\lambda^* y.N[x := y])\\ &\qquad \text{by IH twice}\\ &\equiv \lambda^* y.M[x := y]N[x := y]\\ &\equiv \lambda^* y.(MN)[x := y]\end{aligned}$$

□

The theory CL describes intensional equality between terms (recall the discussion of this issue for λ); to capture extensional equality, we add the following rule (to get the theory CL + **ext**):

$$\frac{Px = P'x}{P = P'} \qquad \text{where } x \notin FV(PP') \qquad \textbf{(ext)}$$

The addition of this rule gives the theory a number of new (useful) properties:

(1) $CL + \textbf{ext} \vdash \mathbf{K} = \lambda^* xy.x$
(2) $CL + \textbf{ext} \vdash \mathbf{S} = \lambda^* xyz.xz(yz)$
(3) $CL + \textbf{ext}$ is closed under the rule:

$$\frac{P = Q}{\lambda^* x.P = \lambda^* x.Q}$$

(recall the weak extensionality rule, ξ, of λ)

Lemma 4.11

$CL + \textbf{ext} \vdash \mathbf{K} = \lambda^* xy.x$

Proof

$$\lambda^* xy.x \equiv \lambda^* x.\mathbf{K}x \equiv \mathbf{S}(\lambda^* x.\mathbf{K})(\lambda^* x.x) \equiv \mathbf{S}(\mathbf{KK})\mathbf{I}$$

which is a normal form CL-term distinct from $\mathbf{K}$; however, using **ext** allows the formula to be proved, since:

$$\begin{aligned}\mathbf{S}(\mathbf{KK})\mathbf{I}xy &= \mathbf{KK}x(\mathbf{I}x)y\\ &= \mathbf{K}(\mathbf{I}x)y\\ &= \mathbf{I}x\\ &= x\\ &= \mathbf{K}xy\end{aligned}$$

□

The second property is proved in a similar way.

Exercise 4.1.5   *1. What is the CL-term corresponding to $\lambda^* xyz.xz(yz)$?*
2. Verify that $CL + \mathbf{ext} \vdash \mathbf{S} = \lambda^* xyz.xz(yz)$

The proof of the third property is as follows:

Lemma 4.12 $CL + \mathbf{ext}$ *is closed under the rule:*

$$\frac{P = Q}{\lambda^* x.P = \lambda^* x.Q}$$

Proof
Suppose $P = Q$. From Lemma 4.7 above, $P = (\lambda^* x.P)x$ and $Q = (\lambda^* x.Q)x$.
Therefore $(\lambda^* x.P)x = (\lambda^* x.Q)x$ but, since $x \notin FV(\lambda^* x.P)$ and $x \notin FV(\lambda^* x.Q)$ by Lemma 4.6, then by **ext**:

$$\lambda^* x.P = \lambda^* x.Q$$

$\square$

We now turn to reduction in Combinatory Logic. There are two notions of reduction for Combinatory Logic. The notion of *weak* reduction, w, is defined in the expected way:

$$w = \{(\mathbf{K}MN, M) \mid M, N \in \mathcal{C}\} \cup \{(\mathbf{S}MNP, MP(NP)) \mid M, N, P \in \mathcal{C}\}$$

The other notion, *strong* reduction, has a rather complicated definition and we will not consider it further except to note that it is equivalent to $\beta\eta$-reduction in the λ-calculus (which has a rather straightforward definition!). From w we can define $\to_w$, $\twoheadrightarrow_w$ and $=_w$ as in Chapter 3. $\twoheadrightarrow_w$ is rightly called "weak" reduction because it does not go "as far as" β-reduction; for example $\mathbf{SK}$ is a w-nf but the corresponding λ-term, $(\lambda xyz.xz(yz))(\lambda xy.x)$, is not a β-nf. Otherwise, we have results for w which are similar to β:

- $M =_w N \Leftrightarrow CL \vdash M = N$
- w is CR

The Church–Rosser Theorem for Combinatory Logic is formally stated as follows:

Theorem 4.13 (Church–Rosser)
(i) If $CL \vdash M = N$ then $\exists Z \in \mathcal{C}.M \twoheadrightarrow_w Z$ and $N \twoheadrightarrow_w Z$
(ii) If $CL \vdash M = N$ and N is a w-nf then $M \twoheadrightarrow_w N$

The definition of the weak-reduction graph of a CL-term M, $G_w(M)$, is analogous to the definition of reduction graphs for λ-terms.

4.2   Combinatory Logic and the λ-calculus

We now turn to a more detailed consideration of the relationship between Combinatory Logic and the λ-calculus. We start by providing translations between CL-terms and λ-terms.

Definition 4.14

$$_{-\lambda} : \mathcal{C} \to \Lambda$$

$$
\begin{aligned}
x_\lambda &\equiv x \\
\mathbf{K}_\lambda &\equiv \lambda xy.x \\
\mathbf{S}_\lambda &\equiv \lambda xyz.xz(yz) \\
(MN)_\lambda &\equiv M_\lambda N_\lambda
\end{aligned}
$$

$$_{-CL} : \Lambda \to \mathcal{C}$$

$$
\begin{aligned}
x_{CL} &\equiv x \\
(MN)_{CL} &\equiv M_{CL}N_{CL} \\
(\lambda x.M)_{CL} &\equiv \lambda^* x.M_{CL}
\end{aligned}
$$

Given our earlier remarks about the use of combinators as machine code, notice that $_{-CL}$ is a prototype compiler for λ-terms. As an example, consider:

Example 4.15

$$
\begin{aligned}
(\lambda xy.xyy)_{CL} &\equiv \lambda^* x.\lambda^* y.xyy \\
&\equiv \lambda^* x.\mathbf{S}(\lambda^* y.xy)(\lambda^* y.y) \\
&\equiv \lambda^* x.\mathbf{S}(\mathbf{S}(\lambda^* y.x)(\lambda^* y.y))\mathbf{I} \\
&\equiv \lambda^* x.\mathbf{S}(\mathbf{S}(\mathbf{K}x)\mathbf{I})\mathbf{I} \\
&\equiv \ldots \\
&\equiv \mathbf{S}(\mathbf{S}(\mathbf{KS})(\mathbf{S}(\mathbf{S}(\mathbf{KS})(\mathbf{S}(\mathbf{KK})\mathbf{I}))(\mathbf{KI})))(\mathbf{KI})
\end{aligned}
$$

Exercise 4.2.1 *Fill in the missing steps ($\ldots$).*

The compiler is not very efficient! The size of the combinator code grows exponentially in the number of arguments of the original term. However, David Turner has successfully used an optimised and extended version of $_{-CL}$ to compile Miranda[2]; his compiler is very sophisticated but there is quite an improvement just using optimisations based on the following four equivalences:

(1) $\mathbf{S}(\mathbf{K}M)\mathbf{I} \equiv M$
(2) $\mathbf{S}(\mathbf{K}M)(\mathbf{K}N) \equiv \mathbf{K}(MN)$
(3) $\mathbf{S}(\mathbf{K}M)N \equiv \mathbf{B}MN$
(4) $\mathbf{S}M(\mathbf{K}N) \equiv \mathbf{C}MN$

---

[2]Miranda is a trademark of Research Software Ltd.

Since the left hand sides of these equivalences overlap (for example any term which matches the second will also match the third and fourth) it is important that the rules are applied (exhaustively) in order. The rules are justified because if we replace $\equiv$ by $=$, then each of the resultant formulae is a theorem in $CL + \mathbf{ext}$. For example, consider:

$\mathbf{S(KM)I}x$ where x is a new variable (i.e. $x \notin FV(M)$)
$= (\mathbf{KM})x(\mathbf{I}x)$
$= M(\mathbf{I}x)$
$= Mx$

and therefore:

$$\mathbf{S}(\mathbf{K}M)\mathbf{I} = M \text{ by } \mathbf{ext}$$

Exercise 4.2.2 *Justify the other three rules in a similar way*

We now return to Example 4.15 and "re-compile" it using the optimisations:

$$\begin{aligned}
\lambda^* x.\mathbf{S}(\mathbf{S}(\mathbf{K}x)\mathbf{I})\mathbf{I} &\equiv \lambda^* x.\mathbf{S}x\mathbf{I} \\
&\equiv \mathbf{S}(\lambda^* x.\mathbf{S}x)(\lambda^* x.\mathbf{I}) \\
&\equiv \mathbf{S}(\mathbf{S}(\lambda^* x.\mathbf{S})(\lambda^* x.x))(\mathbf{KI}) \\
&\equiv \mathbf{S}(\mathbf{S}(\mathbf{KS})\mathbf{I})(\mathbf{KI}) \\
&\equiv \mathbf{SS}(\mathbf{KI}) \\
&\equiv \mathbf{CSI}
\end{aligned}$$

a considerable improvement!

We now have a more rigorous way of generating the definitions for $\mathbf{B}$, $\mathbf{C}$ and $\mathbf{Y}$ which were introduced earlier. For example for $\mathbf{B}$ (missing a few steps which the reader should fill in):

$$\begin{aligned}
(\lambda xyz.x(yz))_{CL} &\equiv \lambda^* xyz.x(yz) \\
&\equiv \lambda^* xy.\mathbf{S}(\mathbf{K}x)(\mathbf{S}(\mathbf{K}y)\mathbf{I}) \\
&\equiv \lambda^* xy.\mathbf{S}(\mathbf{K}x)y \\
&\equiv \lambda^* x.\mathbf{S}(\mathbf{K}(\mathbf{S}(\mathbf{K}x)))\mathbf{I} \\
&\equiv \lambda^* x.\mathbf{S}(\mathbf{K}x) \\
&\equiv \mathbf{S}(\mathbf{KS})(\mathbf{S}(\mathbf{KK})\mathbf{I}) \\
&\equiv \mathbf{S}(\mathbf{KS})\mathbf{K}
\end{aligned}$$

Exercise 4.2.3
(a) use the unoptimised $\_{CL}$ translation to translate $\lambda xyz.xzy$
(b) repeat (a) using the first three optimisations from above.

We now return to a more formal treatment of the relationship between the two theories. First we have the following result:

Proposition 4.16

$$CL \vdash P = Q \Rightarrow \lambda \vdash P_\lambda = Q_\lambda$$

Proof

(induction on the length of the proof of $P = Q$)

(i) $P \equiv \mathbf{S}ABC$ and $Q \equiv AC(BC)$:

$$P_\lambda \equiv \mathbf{S}_\lambda A_\lambda B_\lambda C_\lambda$$
$$\equiv (\lambda xyz.xz(yz))A_\lambda B_\lambda C_\lambda$$
$$= A_\lambda C_\lambda (B_\lambda C_\lambda)$$
$$\equiv Q_\lambda$$

(ii) $P \equiv \mathbf{K}AB$ and $Q \equiv A$: similar to (i).

(iii) $P \equiv Q$: trivial

(iv) $P = Q$ because $Q = P$: trivial

(v) $P = Q$ because $P = R$ and $R = Q$:
By IH $P_\lambda = R_\lambda$ and $R_\lambda = Q_\lambda$ and thus $P_\lambda = Q_\lambda$ by the transitivity of convertibility.

(vi) $P \equiv MZ$ and $Q \equiv NZ$ and $P = Q$ because $M = N$:
$P_\lambda \equiv M_\lambda Z_\lambda = N_\lambda Z_\lambda$ by IH and the corresponding rule of $\lambda \equiv Q_\lambda$

(vii) $P \equiv ZM$ and $Q \equiv ZN$ and $P = Q$ because $M = N$: similar to (vi) $\square$

However the converse is not true: $\lambda \vdash P = Q$ does not imply $CL \vdash P_{CL} = Q_{CL}$. This is because equality in CL is equivalent to w-convertibility; terms in w-nf are distinguished whereas the equivalent λ-terms may be (β-)convertible. An example is the formula $\mathbf{SK} = \mathbf{KI}$; the formula is a theorem of the λ-calculus but not of Combinatory Logic. Curry showed that by adding five extra axioms to CL the resulting theory is equivalent to the λ-calculus. Curry's axioms are:

- $\mathbf{K} = \mathbf{S(S(KS)(S(KK)K))(K(SKK))}$
- $\mathbf{S} = \mathbf{S(S(KS)(S(K(S(KS)))(S(K(S(KK)))S)))(K(K(SKK)))}$
- $\mathbf{S(S(KS)(S(KK)(S(KS)K)))(KK) = S(KK)}$
- $\mathbf{S(KS)(S(KK)) = S(KK)(S(S(KS)(S(KK)(SKK)))(K(SKK)))}$
- $\mathbf{S(K(S(KS)))(S(KS)(S(KS))) =}$
  $\mathbf{S(S(KS)(S(KK)(S(KS)(S(K(S(KS)))S)))) (KS)}$

We will not attempt to justify these axioms here but encourage the interested reader to consult Chapter 7 of Barendregt's book.

Finally, we remark that the translation schemes do not preserve reduction or normal forms. For example, define $\omega \equiv \mathbf{SII}$ (which is just $(\lambda x.xx)_{CL}$) and define $P \equiv \mathbf{S(K}\omega)(\mathbf{K}\omega)$; then P is a w-nf but P_λ is convertible with $\lambda x.\Omega$ which is reducible and does not even have a normal form[3]. A second example is:

$$\lambda x.\mathbf{II} \rightarrow_\beta \lambda x.\mathbf{I}$$

but:

$$\mathbf{S(KI)(KI)}$$

does not weak reduce to **KI**.

4.3 Bases

Definition 4.17 *Suppose that X is a subset of Λ. The set of terms generated by X, written X^+, is the least set Y such that:*

(1) $X \subseteq Y$
(2) $M, N \in Y \Rightarrow (MN) \in Y$

Thus X^+ contains X and is closed under application.

Definition 4.18 *If A is a set of λ-terms, then X (also a set of λ-terms) is a* basis *for A if:*

$$\forall M \in A.\exists N \in X^+.N = M$$

X is called a basis *if X is a basis for Λ^0.*

Proposition 4.19 *The λ-terms corresponding to $\mathbf{K}$ and $\mathbf{S}$ form a basis:*

Proof
First we note that $M_{CL,\lambda} = M$, we will prove this result (in a slightly different context) in Chapter 5.

Clearly if P is a closed CL-term, then $P_\lambda \in \{\mathbf{K}, \mathbf{S}\}^+$.

Now suppose that M is a closed λ-term. Then M_{CL} is a closed CL-term and hence $M_{CL,\lambda} \in \{\mathbf{K}, \mathbf{S}\}^+$.   □

We can actually make the stronger statement:

$$\forall M \in \Lambda^0.\exists N \in \{\mathbf{K}, \mathbf{S}\}^+.N \twoheadrightarrow M$$

It is interesting (but maybe not very useful) to note that there is actually a one element basis consisting of the λ-term:

$$X \equiv \lambda z.z\mathbf{KSK}$$

This is a basis since we have:

$$\mathbf{K} = XXX$$
$$\mathbf{S} = X(XX)$$

In justification of this last statement, we have:

---

[3]There is a good correspondence between *w*-nfs and the weak head normal forms used in lazy evaluation. $\lambda x.\Omega$ is a whnf.

$$XXX = X\mathbf{KSK}X$$
$$= \mathbf{KKSKSK}X$$
$$= \mathbf{KKSK}X$$
$$= \mathbf{KK}X$$
$$= \mathbf{K}$$

Exercise 4.3.1 *Give a similar justification for the statement about* **S**.

4.4   Summary

In this chapter, we have presented a new theory CL. Combinatory Logic was introduced to fulfil the same role as the λ-calculus. The notions that we have studied in the preceding chapters are equally applicable to Combinatory Logic; since we have studied these in detail for the λ-calculus we have merely sketched them in this chapter. We have investigated the relationship between the two theories; as part of this we have seen a prototype compiler for functional languages to combinatory code. We have seen that equality in CL is weaker than β-convertibility. The notion of weak reduction appears to correspond well with lazy reduction. We concluded this chapter by introducing the notion of a basis — a generating set for closed λ-terms; remarkably there is a two-element basis which consists of the two λ-terms: $\lambda xyz.xz(yz)$ and $\lambda xy.x$ — all closed λ-terms can be constructed from these two terms using application. Even more remarkably, every closed λ-term can be constructed by self-application of the term:

$$\lambda z.z(\lambda xy.x)(\lambda xyz.xz(yz))(\lambda xy.x)$$

5

Semantics

Overview

We now make a brief excursion into the model theory of the λ-calculus. We start by abstracting the common properties of models. A detailed study would quickly take us into the realms of domain theory and out of the scope of this book. However, to make the material more concrete, we do consider two model constructions. The first is the term models. We also introduce Böhm trees and show how a model can be constructed from them.

5.1 Models

The purpose of a model is to give a semantics for terms. The objective is to identify each term with an element of some mathematical structure, normally a set or a set with additional structure (e.g. a complete partial order); the underlying theory of the mathematical structure then becomes available as a basis for reasoning about the terms of our language and their inter-relationships.

For the propositional calculus, the "standard" model interprets wff by truth values. A model is a triple:

$$\mathcal{M} = (\mathcal{V}, \mathbf{not}, \mathbf{or})$$

where the first component is a set, and the other two are operations on the set (**not** is unary, the other is binary). The intention is, of course, that these operations will be used to interpret the propositional connectives.

The meanings of wffs are given via an *interpretation* which maps terms to elements of the model. Formally the type of an interpretation for the propositional calculus is given by:

$$[\![\text{-}]\!]^{\mathcal{M}}_{\text{-}} : \mathcal{W} \to (\mathit{Var} \to \mathcal{V}) \to \mathcal{V}$$

The second parameter is an *environment* which maps variables to objects in the model[1]. Interpretations are defined inductively according to the structure of wffs; the reader who is already familiar with denotational semantics will recognise that interpretations are precisely the semantic equa-

---

[1]In the programming literature, environments are variously called association lists, valuations, environments, ... Barendregt uses "valuations" but we have chosen to maintain consistency with the (denotational) semantics literature and use "environments".

tions used there. For the propositional calculus (refer to Chapter 2 for the syntax of the propositional calculus), we have:

$$\begin{aligned}
[\![p]\!]^{\mathcal{M}}\rho &= \rho(p) \\
[\![\neg A]\!]^{\mathcal{M}}\rho &= \mathbf{not}([\![A]\!]^{\mathcal{M}}\rho) \\
[\![(A \vee B)]\!]^{\mathcal{M}}\rho &= ([\![A]\!]^{\mathcal{M}}\rho) \ \mathbf{or} \ ([\![B]\!]^{\mathcal{M}}\rho)
\end{aligned}$$

If we take $\mathcal{M}$ as:

$$\mathcal{V} = \{false, \ true\}$$

$$\begin{aligned}
\mathbf{not} \ false &= true \\
\mathbf{not} \ true &= false
\end{aligned}$$

$$\begin{aligned}
false \ \mathbf{or} \ false &= false \\
false \ \mathbf{or} \ true &= true \\
true \ \mathbf{or} \ false &= true \\
true \ \mathbf{or} \ true &= true
\end{aligned}$$

the interpretation gives the expected truth values to wff.

For the type-free λ-calculus, we are unable to give a (naive) set-theoretic model. The problem is that terms serve as both functions and arguments; in particular, a term can be applied to itself — recall Ω (see Chapter 3). Consequently, a model of the type-free λ-calculus requires a structure which is isomorphic (has the same structure) as its own function space, i.e. we have to "solve" the following:

$$D \cong D \to D$$

In set theory, the only solutions are trivial (D is a singleton) which follows from consideration of the cardinalities of the sets involved. Other than the term models (see below), there were no models of the type-free λ-calculus until the late 1960s. Dana Scott realised that the isomorphism could be solved by imposing a topology on the sets and then restricting the function space to continuous functions with respect to the topology. This fundamental contribution has become known as Scott's thesis:

Scott's Thesis: All computable functions are continuous.

which has a similar status in domain theory to the Church–Turing Thesis. Scott's original work used complete lattices, his first model was called D_∞ and later he published the graph model $P\omega$. Later work in this area has tended to use sub-categories of complete partial orders[2].

A detailed treatment of any particular model, other than the term models, takes us a little far from our main theme; the interested reader is referred to any of the excellent books on this subject which are cited in the

---

[2]One motivation for this switch is that there is often no good computational interpretation for the Top elements which appear in the complete lattice approach.

bibliography. Instead, we will give an abstract characterisation of a model and sketch the construction of the Böhm Tree model. We will introduce two classes of models:

- λ-algebras which satisfy all provable equations of the λ-calculus
- λ-models which satisfy all provable equations of the λ-calculus and the axiom of weak extensionality:

$$\forall x.(M = N) \Rightarrow \lambda x.M = \lambda x.N$$

5.1.1 λ-algebras

We will start with a very simple structure and successively refine it. At the very minimum, we will require a set of objects and an operation on these objects which will be used to give a semantics to application:

Definition 5.1 (Applicative Structure)
$\mathcal{M} = (X, \bullet)$ *is an* applicative structure *if* $\bullet$ *is a binary operation on* X *(i.e.* $\bullet : X \times X \to X$*).*
$\mathcal{M}$ *is said to be* extensional *if, in addition, for* $a, b \in X$*, one has:*

$$(\forall x \in X.a \bullet x = b \bullet x) \Rightarrow a = b$$

We will usually elide the $\bullet$ thus:

$$ax \equiv a \bullet x$$

The class of terms over an applicative structure $\mathcal{T}(\mathcal{M})$ are words over the alphabet:

$$\begin{aligned}
&v_0, v_1, \ldots && \text{variables} \\
&c_a, c_b, \ldots && \text{constants denoting objects in } X \\
&(,) && \text{parentheses}
\end{aligned}$$

Definition 5.2 (Terms)
$\mathcal{T}(\mathcal{M})$ *is the least class satisfying the following:*

(1) $v \in \mathcal{T}(\mathcal{M})$, *v a variable*
(2) $c_a \in \mathcal{T}(\mathcal{M})$, $a \in X$
(3) *if* $A, B \in \mathcal{T}(\mathcal{M})$ *then* $(AB) \in \mathcal{T}(\mathcal{M})$

Before we can give an interpretation to terms in $\mathcal{T}(\mathcal{M})$, we need another definition. Terms can contain free variables and in order to decide what such a term denotes, we must know the "value" of the free variables. In the LISP meta-circular interpreter, this problem is solved by maintaining an *association list* of (name,value) pairs. In the abstract machines of Chapter 8 the problem is solved by maintaining an *environment*. Equivalently, we will use an environment function:

$$\rho : variables \to X$$

An interpretation of $A \in \mathcal{T}(\mathcal{M})$ in $\mathcal{M}$ under ρ – written $[\![A]\!]_\rho^{\mathcal{M}}$ but we will omit ρ and the $\mathcal{M}$-superscript when they are clear from the context – is defined as follows:

$$
\begin{aligned}
[\![v]\!]_\rho^{\mathcal{M}} &= \rho(v) \\
[\![c_a]\!]_\rho^{\mathcal{M}} &= a \\
[\![(AB)]\!]_\rho^{\mathcal{M}} &= [\![A]\!]_\rho^{\mathcal{M}} [\![B]\!]_\rho^{\mathcal{M}}
\end{aligned}
$$

We will write:

$$
\mathcal{M}, \rho \models A = B
$$

read "$A = B$ is true in $\mathcal{M}$ under ρ" if:

$$
[\![A]\!]_\rho^{\mathcal{M}} = [\![B]\!]_\rho^{\mathcal{M}}
$$

(We write $\mathcal{M} \models A = B$ and say "$A = B$ is true in $\mathcal{M}$" if

$$
\mathcal{M}, \rho \models A = B \text{ for all } \rho)
$$

So much for the basic structure; we will now start to refine it. We make the following definition:

Definition 5.3 (Combinatory Algebra)
A combinatory algebra *is an applicative structure with two distinguished elements:*

$$
\mathcal{M} = (X, \bullet, k, s)
$$

which satisfy:

$$
kxy = x
$$

and

$$
sxyz = xz(yz)
$$

A structure is non-trivial if its cardinality is greater than 1; a combinatory algebra is non-trivial if and only if $k \neq s$ (recall the discussion of consistency in Chapter 2). As Barendregt remarks, the use of the word "algebra" is slightly misleading since combinatory algebras do not have many algebraic properties, in particular:

non-trivial combinatory algebras are never commutative:
Define $i = skk$, which behaves as an identity and suppose that the algebra is commutative; then $ik(=k) = ki$ and so:

$$
a = kab = kiab = ib = b
$$

for all a, b - this contradicts the non-triviality assumption!

non-trivial combinatory algebras are never associative:
Suppose the algebra is associative, then $(ki)i = k(ii)(= ki)$ and:

$$
(ki)ia = ia = a \text{ and } kia = i
$$

Thus $a = i$ for all a — contradiction!

non-trivial combinatory algebras are never finite:
Since we can define an infinite sequence of distinct objects:

$$k_1 \quad = k$$
$$\vdots$$
$$k_{n+1} = kk_n$$

Lemma 5.4 *For all* $n, 1 \leq m \leq n+1$ k_{n+2} *is incompatible with* k_m.

Proof
Basis: Suppose that $kk = k$ then $kkiia = kiia$ and thus $i = a$ for all a — contradiction!.

Inductive step: We consider two cases:

(i) $m = 1$: Then $k_{l+3} = k$ implies that $k_{l+3}ab = kab$ and thus $k_{l+1} = a$ for all a — contradiction!

(ii) $m > 1$: Then $k_{l+3} = k_m$ implies $k_{l+3}a = k_ma$ and thus $k_{l+2} = k_{m-1}$. But the latter two terms are incompatible by the IH.

$\square$

non-trivial combinatory algebras are never recursive:
The problem of determining the equality of two objects in the algebra is undecidable (see later).

A simple example of a combinatory algebra is the term model for combinatory logic. Recall that the $=$ relation defined on CL-terms by the theory CL is an equivalence and that it thus partitions $\mathcal{C}$. The term model for CL, denoted by $\mathcal{T}$, is defined by:
$$\mathcal{T} = < \mathcal{C}/_=, \bullet, [\mathbf{S}]_{CL}, [\mathbf{K}]_{CL} >$$
where
$[M]_{CL} = \{N \in \mathcal{C} \mid M = N \text{ is a theorem in } CL\}$
$\mathcal{C}/_= = \{[M]_{CL} \mid M \in \mathcal{C}\}$
$[M]_{CL} \bullet [N]_{CL} = [MN]_{CL}$
Since CL is consistent, in particular $\mathbf{S} = \mathbf{K}$ is not a theorem, $\mathcal{T}$ is a non-trivial model.

Exercise 5.1.1 *Prove the following result using structural induction.*
For all closed terms M, for all environments ρ :
$[\![M]\!]_\rho^{\mathcal{T}} = [M]_{CL}$

An arbitrary applicative structure is capable of modelling application of λ-terms but we have no obvious way of representing abstraction terms. In a combinatory algebra, it is possible to simulate abstraction and thus combinatory algebras are candidate models for the λ-calculus. However, we shall see later, that in an arbitrary combinatory algebra, some of the equations we expect to be true fail to hold; this will force us to refine the structure still further. But first, we remind the reader how to simulate abstraction. We start by extending the class of terms with three distinguished constants, $\mathbf{K}$ and $\mathbf{S}$, which denote k and s respectively and $\mathbf{I}$ which denotes $s \bullet k \bullet k$. For $A \in \mathcal{T}(\mathcal{M})$ and variable x, we define the term $\lambda^* x.A \in \mathcal{T}(\mathcal{M})$ as in Chapter 4:

Definition 5.5

$$\begin{aligned}
\lambda^* x.x &\equiv \mathbf{I} \\
\lambda^* x.P &\equiv \mathbf{K}P, \textit{if } P \textit{ does not contain } x \\
\lambda^* x.PQ &\equiv \mathbf{S}(\lambda^* x.P)(\lambda^* x.Q)
\end{aligned}$$

We have already seen that λ^* does capture the main properties of abstraction. We extend the class of λ-terms, Λ, to $\Lambda(\mathcal{M})$ which consist of the λ-terms built from variables and constants from $\mathcal{M}$. We now define two maps which establish a relationship between $\Lambda(\mathcal{M})$ and the terms over $\mathcal{M}$; notice that these are similar to the maps defined in Chapter 4 except we also deal with constants:

Definition 5.6 ($_{CL}$ **and** $_{\lambda}$)
$_{CL} : \Lambda(\mathcal{M}) \to \mathcal{T}(\mathcal{M})$

$$\begin{aligned}
x_{CL} &= x \\
c_{CL} &= c \\
(MN)_{CL} &= M_{CL}N_{CL} \\
(\lambda x.M)_{CL} &= \lambda^* x.M_{CL}
\end{aligned}$$

$_{\lambda} : \mathcal{T}(\mathcal{M}) \to \Lambda(\mathcal{M})$

$$\begin{aligned}
x_{\lambda} &= x \\
c_{\lambda} &= c \\
\mathbf{I}_{\lambda} &= \lambda x.x \\
\mathbf{K}_{\lambda} &= \lambda xy.x \\
\mathbf{S}_{\lambda} &= \lambda xyz.xz(yz) \\
(AB)_{\lambda} &= A_{\lambda}B_{\lambda}
\end{aligned}$$

Since we are mainly interested in λ-terms, we will abuse notation and write M when we should write M_{CL} and use the turnstile, $\models$, for equality between λ-terms:

$$\mathcal{M}, \rho \models M = N \equiv [\![M_{CL}]\!]_{\rho}^{\mathcal{M}} = [\![N_{CL}]\!]_{\rho}^{\mathcal{M}}$$

$$\mathcal{M} \models M = N \equiv [\![M_{CL}]\!]^{\mathcal{M}} = [\![N_{CL}]\!]^{\mathcal{M}} \text{ for all } \rho$$

Definition 5.7 (λ-algebra)
A combinatory algebra is called a λ-algebra if for all $A, B \in \mathcal{T}(\mathcal{M})$:

$$\lambda \vdash A_\lambda = B_\lambda \Rightarrow \mathcal{M} \models A = B$$

Not all combinatory algebras are λ-algebras; for example in the term model for combinatory logic:

$$\mathcal{M} \not\models \mathbf{S(KI)I = I}$$

while:

$$
\begin{aligned}
(\mathbf{S(KI)I})_\lambda &= (\lambda xyz.xz(yz))((\lambda xy.x)(\lambda x.x))(\lambda x.x) \\
&= (\lambda yz.((\lambda xy.x)(\lambda x.x))z(yz))(\lambda x.x) \\
&= \lambda z.((\lambda xy.x)(\lambda x.x))z((\lambda x.x)z) \\
&= \lambda z.(\lambda y.(\lambda x.x))z((\lambda x.x)z) \\
&= \lambda z.(\lambda x.x)((\lambda x.x)z) \\
&= \lambda z.(\lambda x.x)z \\
&= \lambda x.x \\
&= \mathbf{I}_\lambda
\end{aligned}
$$

We now give a theorem which gives a slightly more useful characterisation of λ-algebras:

Theorem 5.8 *Let $\mathcal{M}$ be a combinatory algebra, then $\mathcal{M}$ is a λ-algebra iff:*
$\forall M, N \in \Lambda(\mathcal{M})$
   1. $\lambda \vdash M = N \Rightarrow \mathcal{M} \models M = N$
   2. $\mathcal{M} \models \mathbf{K}_{\lambda,CL} = \mathbf{K}$ and $\mathcal{M} \models \mathbf{S}_{\lambda,CL} = \mathbf{S}$

Proof
($\Rightarrow$)
First we prove, by an induction on the structure of M, that for all $M \in \Lambda(\mathcal{M})$:

$$\lambda \vdash M_{CL,\lambda} = M$$

- M a variable or constant, say x:

$$x_{CL,\lambda} = (x_{CL})_\lambda = x_\lambda = x$$

- M an application, (PQ):

$$(PQ)_{CL,\lambda} = P_{CL,\lambda}Q_{CL,\lambda} = PQ_{CL,\lambda} \text{ by IH } = PQ \text{ by IH}$$

- M an abstraction, $\lambda x.P$:
We require an induction over the body of the abstraction to show that:

$$(\lambda^* x.P_{CL})_\lambda = \lambda x.P_{CL,\lambda}$$

and the result follows from the outer IH. There are 3 cases:

(i) $P \equiv x$

$$(\lambda^* x.x)_\lambda = \mathbf{S}_\lambda \mathbf{K}_\lambda \mathbf{K}_\lambda$$
$$= (\lambda xyz.xz(yz))(\lambda xy.x)(\lambda xy.x)$$
$$= (\lambda z.(\lambda xy.x)z((\lambda xy.x)z))$$
$$= \lambda x.x$$

(ii) P does not contain x

$$(\mathbf{K}P_{CL})_\lambda = \mathbf{K}_\lambda P_{CL,\lambda} = (\lambda yx.y)P_{CL,\lambda} = \lambda x.P_{CL,\lambda}$$

(iii) $P \equiv QR$

$$(\mathbf{S}(\lambda^* x.Q_{CL})(\lambda^* x.R_{CL}))_\lambda = \mathbf{S}_\lambda(\lambda x.Q_{CL,\lambda})(\lambda x.R_{CL,\lambda}) \text{ by IH twice}$$
$$= \lambda z.Q_{CL,\lambda}[x := z]R_{CL,\lambda}[x := z]$$
$$= \lambda x.Q_{CL,\lambda}R_{CL,\lambda}$$
$$= \lambda x.(QR)_{CL,\lambda}$$

Now we return to the main proof:

(1)

$$\lambda \vdash M = N \Rightarrow \lambda \vdash M_{CL,\lambda} = N_{CL,\lambda} \text{ by the above result}$$
$$\Rightarrow \mathcal{M} \models M_{CL} = N_{CL} \text{ since } \mathcal{M} \text{ is a } \lambda\text{-algebra}$$
$$\Rightarrow \mathcal{M} \models M = N \text{ by definition}$$

(2) By the above result, we have that for all $A \in \mathcal{T}(\mathcal{M})$:

$$\lambda \vdash A_{\lambda,CL,\lambda} = A_\lambda$$

and thus, since $\mathcal{M}$ is a λ-algebra:

$$\mathcal{M} \models A_{\lambda,CL} = A$$

($\Leftarrow$)

We start by proving that:

$$\mathcal{M} \models A_{\lambda,CL} = A$$

for $A \in \mathcal{T}(\mathcal{M})$. We use induction over the structure of A:

- $A \equiv x$ or $A \equiv c$: trivial
- $A \equiv \mathbf{K}$ or $A \equiv \mathbf{S}$: follows from (2)
- $A \equiv PQ$: $(PQ)_{\lambda,CL} = P_{\lambda,CL}Q_{\lambda,CL}$ and the result follows by a double application of the IH.

Now:

$$\lambda \vdash A_\lambda = B_\lambda \Rightarrow \mathcal{M} \models A_{\lambda,CL} = B_{\lambda,CL} \text{ by (1)}$$
$$\Rightarrow \mathcal{M} \models A = B \text{ by the above result}$$

$\square$

5.1.2 λ-models

Finally, we arrive at the most natural class of models: the λ-models. Given a combinatory algebra, we define:

$$\mathbf{1} = s(ki)$$

A good intuition is that $\mathbf{1}$ is a function application operator — it takes two arguments and applies the first to the second.

Definition 5.9 (λ-model)
A λ-model is a λ-algebra, M, in which the following axiom, due to Meyer and Scott, holds:

$$\forall a, b, x \in M.(ax = bx) \Rightarrow \mathbf{1}a = \mathbf{1}b$$

Below, we will give an alternative characterisation of λ-models, but first we need some results about $\mathbf{1}$:

Proposition 5.10 *Let $\mathcal{M}$ be a combinatory algebra, then in $\mathcal{M}$:*
(i) $\mathbf{1}ab = ab$
If, moreover, $\mathcal{M}$ is a λ-algebra then:
(ii) $\mathbf{1} = \lambda xy.xy$
(iii) $\mathbf{1}(\lambda x.A) = \lambda x.A$ for all $A \in \mathcal{T}(\mathcal{M})$
(iv) $\mathbf{11} = \mathbf{1}$

Proof
(i) — (iv) all follow by straightforward manipulation, we illustrate (ii):

$$\begin{aligned}
\mathbf{1}_\lambda &= (\lambda xyz.xz(yz))((\lambda xy.x)(\lambda x.x)) \\
&= (\lambda yz.((\lambda xy.x)(\lambda x.x))z(yz)) \\
&= (\lambda yz.(\lambda y.(\lambda x.x))z(yz)) \\
&= (\lambda yz.(\lambda x.x)(yz)) \\
&= \lambda yz.yz
\end{aligned}$$

$\square$

Exercise 5.1.2 *Complete the above proof.*

A λ-algebra is *weakly extensional* if for $A, B \in \mathcal{T}(\mathcal{M})$:

$$\mathcal{M} \models \forall x.(A = B) \Rightarrow \lambda^* x.A = \lambda^* x.B$$

We close this section with a theorem which characterises λ-models in terms of weakly extensional λ-algebras:

Theorem 5.11 $\mathcal{M}$ *is a λ-model $\Leftrightarrow$ $\mathcal{M}$ is a w.e. λ-algebra*

Proof
($\Leftarrow$)
Let $\mathcal{M}$ be a w.e. λ-algebra, then

$$\forall x.ax = bx \Rightarrow \lambda x.ax = \lambda x.bx$$

$$\Rightarrow 1a = 1b \text{ by (ii) above}$$

($\Rightarrow$)
Let $\mathcal{M}$ be a λ-model, then

$$\forall x.A = B \Rightarrow \forall x.(\lambda x.A)x = (\lambda x.B)x$$

$$\Rightarrow 1(\lambda x.A) = 1(\lambda x.B) \text{ by definition}$$

$$\Rightarrow \lambda x.A = \lambda x.B \text{ by (iii)}$$

$\square$

5.1.3   Term models

Recall that we introduced the term model for Combinatory Logic earlier. The basic idea is that the semantics of a term is given to be the equivalence class of the term under the convertibility relationship.

We define the equivalence class of a term M.

Definition 5.12 $[M] \equiv \{N \in \Lambda \mid \lambda \vdash M = N\}$

As is usual, the equivalence classes partition the set of terms and we can define a quotient set:

$$\Lambda/\lambda \equiv \{[M] \mid M \in \Lambda\}$$

Finally, we can define a binary operation, $\bullet$, on equivalence classes:

$$[M] \bullet [N] \equiv [MN]$$

We now have the necessary components to enable us to define a model.

Definition 5.13 (Term Models)
The open term model for the type free λ-calculus is:

$$\mathcal{M}(\lambda) = (\Lambda/\lambda, \bullet, [\lambda xy.x], [\lambda xyz.xz(yz)])$$

If it is the closed terms that are of interest, we can consider the closed term model:

$$\mathcal{M}^0(\lambda) = (\Lambda^0/\lambda, \bullet, [\lambda xy.x]^0, [\lambda xyz.xz(yz)]^0)$$

We then have the following two facts, which the reader is invited to verify:

Fact 1: $\mathcal{M}^0(\lambda)$ is a λ-algebra

Fact 2: $\mathcal{M}(\lambda)$ is a λ-model

5.2 Böhm Trees

5.2.1 Böhm-like Trees

In this section, we develop a model of the λ-calculus based on a tree representation. We must first develop a suitable representation for trees. Recall that a tree is a collection of nodes; one node, the *root*, is distinguished, each node other than the root has a unique parent and all nodes are reachable from the root. Given these facts, it is clear that any tree can be represented by a set of sequences. Each sequence in the set represents a node in the tree; the sequence records the (unique) path from the root of the tree to the node. For our model, we will require labelled trees (each node will be labelled with a symbol), these are represented by an appropriate (partial) function:

Definition 5.14 (Partially Σ-labelled Trees)
A partially Σ-labelled tree is a partial map:

$$\varphi : Seq \hookrightarrow \Sigma \times N$$

such that:

(1) *$\varphi(\sigma)$ is defined and $\tau < \sigma \Rightarrow \varphi(\tau)$ is defined.*

(2) *$\varphi(\sigma) = <a, n> \Rightarrow \forall k \geq n.\varphi(\sigma * <k>)$ is undefined.*

where *Seq* is the set of sequence numbers which represent paths through the tree[3] and $*$ is the concatenation operator on sequences; Σ is a set of symbols. The intuition behind this definition is that the pair associated with a sequence by φ specifies the symbol associated with the node at the end of the sequence and the arity of the symbol (number of successors). The map φ is partial because the result is undefined if it is applied to an invalid sequence number; this case is handled by the second part of the definition.

We will use a particular set of symbols to label trees:

Definition 5.15 *Let Σ_1 be the set:*

$$\{\lambda x_1 \ldots x_n.y \mid n \geq 0, x_1, \ldots, x_n, y \ \text{variables}\}$$

---

[3]Sequences represent paths through the tree in the following way:
$<>$ is the sequence number of the root,
$< 1 >$ is the first successor of the root,
$< 321 >$ is the first successor of the second successor
of the third successor of the root,

. . . .

The Böhm tree of a λ-term M, $BT(M)$, is defined in the following way:

Definition 5.16 (Böhm Trees)
$BT(M)(\sigma)$ *is undefined for all* σ *if* M *has no hnf.*
If M *has principal hnf* $\lambda x_1 \ldots x_n.yM_0 \ldots M_{m-1}$, *then:*

$$BT(M)(<>) = < \lambda x_1 \ldots x_n.y, m >$$

and for all σ:

$$BT(M)(< k > *\sigma) = BT(M_k)(\sigma) \text{ if } k < m,$$
$$\text{undefined if } k \geq m$$

So the nodes of a Böhm tree record information about the principal hnf of a term and its derivatives. In the following we use $\perp$ to represent the undefined tree. The information that is recorded at each node is similar to the KSL triples of Chapter 8.

Example 5.17

(1) $BT(\mathbf{S}) =$

(2) $BT(\mathbf{S}a\Omega) =$

Definition 5.18
(i) A Böhm-like tree is a partially Σ_1*-labelled tree;* $\mathcal{B}$ *is the set of all Böhm-like trees.*
(ii) $\Lambda\mathcal{B} = \{A \in \mathcal{B} \mid \exists M \in \Lambda.BT(M) = A\}$.
(iii) $A \in \mathcal{B}$ *is* $\perp$*-free iff* $\forall \alpha \in A.A(\alpha)$ *is defined.*

Definition 5.16 defines how a Böhm tree is associated with a particular λ-term. The last definition defines a general set of trees; we now turn to the problem of establishing a relationship between these two notions. It turns out that each finite Böhm-like tree is the Böhm tree of some λ-term; we demonstrate this by the following construction:

Definition 5.19
Let $A \in \mathcal{B}$ *be finite. We define a* λ*-term* M_A *which has* A *as its Böhm tree; the definition is by induction over the depth*[4] *of* A:

---

[4]The depth of a tree is equal to the length of the longest path through the tree.

(1) $A = \bot$: *Take* $M_A \equiv \Omega$.

(2) $A = \lambda\vec{x}.y$: *Take* $M_A \equiv \lambda\vec{x}.y$.

(3) $A =$

$$
\begin{array}{c}
\lambda\vec{x}.y \qquad\quad : \\[2pt]
\diagup\!\!\diagdown \\[-2pt]
A_1 \ldots A_n
\end{array}
$$

Take $M_A \equiv \lambda\vec{x}.y M_{A_1} \ldots M_{A_n}$

Given Böhm-like trees A and B we write:

$$A \subseteq B$$

if and only if A results from B by cutting off some of B's subtrees. From this we can define an ordering between λ-terms:

Definition 5.20 *Let* $M, N \in \Lambda$.
(i) $M \approx N$ *iff* $BT(M) = BT(N)$
(ii) $M \sqsubseteq\!\!\sim N$ *iff* $BT(M) \subseteq BT(N)$

It is easy to verify that the ordering satisfies the following:

Fact: $M \sqsubseteq\!\!\sim N \Rightarrow C[M] \sqsubseteq\!\!\sim C[N]$

Finally, we introduce some notation to represent trees which are uniformly "pruned". The tree A^k is the tree that results from A by cutting off all of the subtrees at depth k:

Definition 5.21
(i) Let $A \in \mathcal{B}$. *For* $k \in N$, *we define:*

$$
\begin{aligned}
A^k(\alpha) &= A(\alpha) \ \ if \ length(\alpha) < k \\
&\quad undefined, \ otherwise
\end{aligned}
$$

(ii) $BT^k(P) = (BT(P))^k$
(iii) $P^{(k)} \equiv M_{BT^k(P)}$
(iv) For $A, B \in \mathcal{B}$, *we write* $A =_k B$ *iff* $A^k = B^k$

5.2.2   The Model $\mathcal{B}$

In this subsection, our aim is to construct a λ-model based on Böhm-like trees. The model, also called $\mathcal{B}$, will satisfy:

$$\mathcal{B} \models M = N \Leftrightarrow BT(M) = BT(N)$$

In the construction of the model we will employ the notion of *limit of an increasing chain* of trees:

$$A_0 \subseteq A_1 \subseteq A_2 \subseteq \ldots$$

We denote the limit by $\bigsqcup A_n$ and define it as follows:

$$\bigsqcup A_n = \bigcup_n A_n$$

It can be shown that every Böhm-like tree is the limit of a chain of finite trees (the trees which result from pruning the tree at successively deeper levels):

$$A = \bigsqcup A^n$$

This notion of limit can be extended to λ-terms: if we have an increasing sequence of terms $\{M_n\}$, then if A is a Böhm-like tree and M is a term, we write:

$$\bigsqcup M_n = A \text{ if } \bigsqcup BT(M_n) = A$$

and:

$$\bigsqcup M_n = M \text{ if } \bigsqcup BT(M_n) = BT(M)$$

depending on whether we are interested in the Böhm-like tree or a term as the limit.

Armed with these notions, we can define a number of useful operations on Böhm-like trees:

Definition 5.22 *Let* $A, B \in \mathcal{B}$. *We define:*
(i) $A \cdot B = AB = \bigsqcup(M_{A^n} M_{B^n})$
(ii) $\lambda x.A = \bigsqcup(\lambda x.M_{A^n})$
(iii) $A(x := B) = \bigsqcup(M_{A^n}[x := M_{B^n}])$

In order for the above definition to be well-formed, we have to verify that the collections of terms used on the right hand sides do indeed form increasing chains (otherwise the limit is not defined). We will verify this for (i):

Lemma 5.23 *For all* $A, B \in \mathcal{B}$, *the set* $\{M_{A^n} M_{B^n}\}$ *is an increasing chain.*

Proof
Clearly $A^n \subseteq A^{n+1}$. Consequently $M_{A^n} \stackrel{\sqsubseteq}{\sim} M_{A^{n+1}}$ since $BT(M_{A^n}) = A^n$. The same holds for the B terms. Hence by two uses of the Fact at the end of the last subsection:

$$M_{A^n} M_{B^n} \stackrel{\sqsubseteq}{\sim} M_{A^{n+1}} M_{B^n} \stackrel{\sqsubseteq}{\sim} M_{A^{n+1}} M_{B^{n+1}}$$

$\square$

Exercise 5.2.1 *Show that the other chains exist.*

We are now ready to define the model. We first spell out the form of an interpretation; this involves a small subtlety in the case for abstractions.

Given a valuation ρ in $\mathcal{B}$, we define the interpretation $[\![\_]\!]_\rho : \Lambda(\mathcal{B}) \to \mathcal{B}$ in the following way:

$$
\begin{aligned}
[\![x]\!]_\rho &= \rho(x) \\
[\![c_A]\!]_\rho &= A \\
[\![PQ]\!]_\rho &= [\![P]\!]_\rho [\![Q]\!]_\rho \\
[\![\lambda x.P]\!]_\rho &= \lambda x.[\![P]\!]_{\rho[x := BT(x)]}
\end{aligned}
$$

where the notation $\rho[x := a]$ is used to represent an environment that is everywhere the same as ρ, except at x which it now maps to a, i.e.:

$$
\begin{aligned}
\rho[x := a](y) &= \rho(y), \text{ if } x \not\equiv y \\
&= a, \text{ otherwise}
\end{aligned}
$$

Then we have:

Fact: $\mathcal{B} = (\mathcal{B}, \cdot)$ is a λ-model

Exercise 5.2.2 *Verify this fact.*

Approach 1: *Verify that $\mathcal{B}$ is a combinatory algebra which is a weakly extensional λ-algebra. This may involve you in proving a large number of subsidiary properties of the operations that we have introduced.*

Approach 2: *Refer to Barendregt's Chapter 18 where an alternative approach is described.*

Finally, we can verify the property that we opened this subsection with:

Theorem 5.24

$$
\mathcal{B} \models M = N \Leftrightarrow BT(M) = BT(N)
$$

Proof

$(\Rightarrow)$

$$
\begin{aligned}
\mathcal{B} \models M = N &\Rightarrow \forall \rho.[\![M]\!]_\rho = [\![N]\!]_\rho \\
&\Rightarrow BT(M) = BT(N) \text{ taking } \rho(y) = BT(y) \text{ for all } y
\end{aligned}
$$

$(\Leftarrow)$

$$
\begin{aligned}
&BT(M) = BT(N) \\
&\Rightarrow \text{ for any substitution for free variables, } (\_), BT(M)(\_) = BT(N)(\_) \\
&\Rightarrow [\![M]\!]_\rho = [\![N]\!]_\rho \\
&\Rightarrow \mathcal{B} \models M = N
\end{aligned}
$$

$\square$

5.3 Summary

In this chapter we have considered the semantics of λ-terms. We have given an abstract formulation of the properties that a model should satisfy and we have given a concrete example of term models for the λ-calculus. We have developed the notion of Böhm trees and shown the construction of a model based on them.

6

Computability

Overview

A classical application of the λ-calculus was in the study of computability. This is the topic of this chapter. Since most computations involve repetitive execution of "code", fixed points (for encoding recursion) play a fundamental rôle; we start by reviewing the Fixed Point Theorem and (re-)introducing the concept of a fixed point combinator. Next, rather than add delta rules for constants (see Chapter 3), we explore how constants can be handled in the pure calculus. We introduce several ways of encoding numerals and functions on them. In the third section, we introduce the notion of λ-*definability* - this allows us to relate the λ-calculus to other formalisms such as Kleene's Recursive Functions and Turing Machines. The final section of this chapter discusses the issue of decidability in the λ-calculus and we present some undecidable problems.

6.1 Fixed Points

In order to study the computability aspects of the λ-calculus, we will rely extensively on the ability to make recursive definitions. In this section we re-introduce the concept of a *fixed point combinator* and consider the variety of different combinators.

We start by recalling the Fixed Point Theorem from Chapter 2:

Theorem 6.1 (The Fixed Point Theorem)

$$\forall F.\exists X.X = FX$$

Proof
Let $W \equiv \lambda x.F(xx)$ and $X \equiv WW$. Then

$$X \equiv (\lambda x.F(xx))W \to F(WW) \equiv FX$$

$\square$

The proof inspires us to make the following definition:

Definition 6.2 (A Fixed Point Combinator)

$$\mathbf{Y} \equiv \lambda f.(\lambda x.f(xx))(\lambda x.f(xx))$$

This is a term which, when applied to another term, is equal to the fixed point of the given term. $\mathbf{Y}$ is sometimes known as Curry's Paradoxical Combinator (consider the result of applying $\mathbf{Y}$ to a term representing logical negation). In general, any term M which satisfies the following:

$$\forall F.MF = F(MF)$$

is called a fixed point combinator; we shall see shortly that there are infinitely many such combinators.

In the preceding paragraph we have used convertibility both in the statement of the Fixed Point Theorem and the definition of fixed point combinators. Sometimes it will be desirable to have a fixed point combinator M which satisfies the slightly stronger requirement:

$$\forall F.MF \twoheadrightarrow F(MF)$$

Notice that $\mathbf{Y}$ does not have this property (check this!) but the following combinator does:

$$\Theta \equiv AA \text{ where } A \equiv \lambda xy.y(xxy)$$

since:

$$\begin{aligned}
\Theta F &\equiv (\lambda xy.y(xxy))AF \\
&\to (\lambda y.y(AAy))F \\
&\to F(AAF) \\
&\equiv F(\Theta F)
\end{aligned}$$

The general definition of fixed point combinators is universally quantified over all terms. The following lemma, which is due to Böhm and van der Mey, characterises fixed point combinators by their interaction with a single term:

Lemma 6.3 (Böhm and van der Mey)
Let $G \equiv \lambda yf.f(yf)(\equiv \mathbf{SI})$
Then $M \in \Lambda$ is a fixed point combinator $\Leftrightarrow M = GM$

Proof
($\Leftarrow$)
If $M = GM$ then:

$$\begin{aligned}
\forall F.MF &= GMF \\
&\equiv (\lambda yf.f(yf))MF \\
&= F(MF)
\end{aligned}$$

i.e. M is a fixed point combinator

($\Rightarrow$)
Suppose M is a fixed point combinator, then:

$$\forall F.MF = F(MF)$$

But then by the Church–Rosser Theorem there is a term to which both MF and $F(MF)$ reduce; any such term must be of the form $F(\ldots)$ since F is arbitrary. For MF to be reducible to such a term, M must be an abstraction, say $\lambda f.N$ for some N. But then:

$$\lambda f.Mf \equiv \lambda f.(\lambda f.N)f = \lambda f.N \equiv M$$

and now notice that:

$$
\begin{aligned}
M &= \lambda f.Mf \\
&= \lambda f.f(Mf) \text{ since } M \text{ is a fixed point combinator} \\
&= GM
\end{aligned}
$$

$\square$

We now have the wherewithal to demonstrate that there is an infinite variety of fixed point combinators. We define a sequence of combinators, thus:

$$
\begin{aligned}
\mathbf{Y}^0 &\equiv \mathbf{Y} \\
\mathbf{Y}^{n+1} &\equiv \mathbf{Y}^n G
\end{aligned}
$$

where G is as defined in the previous lemma

It is clear that the elements of this sequence are all distinct terms. Furthermore, we have the following result.

Lemma 6.4 *All members of the sequence* $\mathbf{Y}^0, \mathbf{Y}^1, \ldots$ *are fixed point combinators:*

Proof
By induction over n, where the basis is trivial (see earlier).
Now:

$$
\begin{aligned}
G\mathbf{Y}^{n+1} &\equiv G(\mathbf{Y}^n G) \\
&= \mathbf{Y}^n G \\
&\quad \text{since } \mathbf{Y}^n \text{ is a fixed point combinator by the IH} \\
&\equiv \mathbf{Y}^{n+1}
\end{aligned}
$$

The result follows by an appeal to the preceding lemma. $\square$

Notice that:

$$\mathbf{Y}^1 \twoheadrightarrow \Theta$$

since:

$$
\begin{aligned}
\mathbf{Y}^1 &\equiv \mathbf{Y}G \\
&\rightarrow (\lambda x.G(xx))(\lambda x.G(xx)) \\
&\rightarrow (\lambda xf.f(xxf))(\lambda x.G(xx)) \\
&\rightarrow (\lambda xf.f(xxf))(\lambda xf.f(xxf)) \\
&\equiv \Theta
\end{aligned}
$$

We now introduce a result which we will make implicit use of throughout the rest of this chapter:

Proposition 6.5 *Let $C \equiv C(f, \vec{x})$ be a term (with free variables f and $\vec{x}$), then:*

(i) $\exists F. \forall \vec{N}. F\vec{N} = C(F, \vec{N})$

(ii) $\exists F. \forall \vec{N}. F\vec{N} \twoheadrightarrow C(F, \vec{N})$

Proof
In both cases, we can take $F \equiv \Theta(\lambda f \vec{x}. C(f, \vec{x}))$. Notice that we could use **Y** instead for (i).   □

Example 6.6 *As an example suppose that:*

$$C \equiv fyxf \equiv C(f, x, y)$$

then (i) guarantees the existence of a term F such that:

$$Fxy = FyxF$$

Just take $F \equiv \Theta(\lambda fxy. fyxf)$ then:

$$
\begin{aligned}
Fxy &\equiv \Theta(\lambda fxy. fyxf)xy \\
&= (\lambda fxy. fyxf)(\Theta(\lambda fxy. fyxf))xy \\
&\equiv (\lambda fxy. fyxf)Fxy \\
&= FyxF
\end{aligned}
$$

Example 6.7 *A more familiar example is:*

$$C \equiv \text{if } n = 0 \text{ then } 1 \text{ else } n \times f(n-1) \equiv C(f, n)$$

and (i) guarantees the existence of a term, F, which behaves like a factorial function[1], i.e.:

$$Fn = \text{if } n = 0 \text{ then } 1 \text{ else } n \times F(n-1)$$

and we just take:

$$F \equiv \mathbf{Y}(\lambda fn. \text{if } n = 0 \text{ then } 1 \text{ else } n \times f(n-1))$$

Finally we recall the definition of the term Ω:

$$\Omega \equiv \omega\omega \text{ where } \omega \equiv \lambda x. xx$$

and just note that[2]:

$$\Omega = \mathbf{YI}$$

---

[1]Of course we have deviated somewhat from the standard syntax for terms but hopefully the message in this example is clear.

[2]Readers familiar with domain theory should consider what the fixed point of the identity function is. Ω is playing the same role as $\bot$ (recall the discussion of head normal forms in Chapter 3).

6.2   Numeral Systems

In the next section we show the equivalence of the λ-calculus and Recursive Function Theory. To do this, we will need to define λ-terms which encode numerals, booleans, conditionals and various other constructs; we shall consider various approaches to this problem in this section.

We start with boolean values. We define true and false by terms **T** and **F**:

Definition 6.8 (True and False)

$$\mathbf{T} \equiv \lambda xy.x \equiv \mathbf{K}$$

$$\mathbf{F} \equiv \lambda xy.y \equiv \mathbf{KI}$$

These choices are motivated by the simple definition of the conditional function which follows:

$$\mathbf{if} \equiv \lambda pca.pca$$

since:

$$\mathbf{if}\ \mathbf{T}MN \twoheadrightarrow M$$

and

$$\mathbf{if}\ \mathbf{F}MN \twoheadrightarrow N$$

There are also simple representations for the standard boolean operations, for example **and**[3]:

$$\mathbf{and} \equiv \lambda xy.xy\mathbf{F}$$

Exercise 6.2.1 *Encode some of the other logical operations using this approach.*

We will also need to manipulate pairs of terms or, more generally, tuples.

Definition 6.9 (Pairs)
We define the pairing operation as a distfix operator, [_, _]:

$$[M, N] \equiv \lambda z.zMN$$

The first and second projection functions on a pair are defined as

$$(\lambda p.p\mathbf{T})$$

---

[3]This encoding uses a trick that is often used in the code generators of compilers, which is to encode the logical operations as conditional expressions. For example **and** x y is equivalent to:

$$\mathbf{if}\ \mathrm{x}\ \mathbf{then}\ \mathrm{y}\ \mathbf{else}\ \mathrm{false}$$

and

$$(\lambda p.p\mathbf{F})$$

respectively.

These definitions are sensible since, for example, if $M \equiv [P, Q]$ then:

$$\begin{aligned} M\mathbf{T} &\equiv (\lambda z.zPQ)\mathbf{T} \\ &\to \mathbf{T}PQ \\ &\twoheadrightarrow P \end{aligned}$$

Ordered n-tuples can now be defined using pairing[4]:

$$[M] \equiv M$$

$$[M_0, \ldots, M_{n+1}] \equiv [M_0, [M_1, \ldots, [M_n, M_{n+1}] \ldots]]$$

The generalisation of the projection functions are defined by the following terms; $\pi_{i,n}$ selects the i-th element from an $n+1$ element tuple, $0 \le i < n$:

$$\pi_{i,n} \equiv \lambda x.x\mathbf{F}^{*i}\mathbf{T} \equiv \lambda x.x\mathbf{F}\ldots(\text{i occurrences of } \mathbf{F})\ldots\mathbf{FT}$$

$$\pi_{n,n} \equiv \lambda x.x\mathbf{F}^{*n}$$

An alternative approach to defining tuples is slightly more direct:

$$< M_0, \ldots, M_n > \equiv \lambda z.zM_0 \ldots M_n$$

and then we define the projection functions as follows:

$$P_{i,n} \equiv \lambda x.xU_{i,n}$$

where

$$U_{i,n} \equiv \lambda x_0 \ldots x_n.x_i$$

Before, we introduce our first numeral system, we need one further combinator, composition, which is written as an infix operator:

$$M \circ N \equiv \lambda x.M(Nx)$$

which is the $\mathbf{B}$ combinator of Combinatory Logic.

We now define the numerals as the following terms:

Definition 6.10 (Standard Numerals)

$$\begin{aligned} \ulcorner 0 \urcorner &\equiv \mathbf{I} \\ \ulcorner n+1 \urcorner &\equiv [\mathbf{F}, \ulcorner n \urcorner] \end{aligned}$$

---

[4]This may remind the reader of dotted pairs in LISP.

So for example:

$$\ulcorner 3 \urcorner \equiv [\mathbf{F}, [\mathbf{F}, [\mathbf{F}, \mathbf{I}]]]$$

This way of constructing numerals is reminiscent of the following type construction:

$$num = Zero \mid Succ\,num$$

in which 3 would be represented as:

$$Succ(Succ(Succ\,Zero))$$

This last consideration motivates the definition of a successor function $\mathbf{S}^+$:

$$\mathbf{S}^+ \equiv \lambda x.[\mathbf{F}, x]$$

The predecessor function, which decrements the numeral by 1, is just the second projection function:

$$\mathbf{P}^- \equiv \lambda x.x\mathbf{F}$$

Notice that:

$$\mathbf{P}^-(\ulcorner 0 \urcorner) \equiv \mathbf{P}^-\mathbf{I} \to \mathbf{IF} \to \mathbf{F}$$

We also define a unary predicate, **Zero**, which returns $\mathbf{T}$ if its argument is $\ulcorner 0 \urcorner$ and $\mathbf{F}$ otherwise:

$$\mathbf{Zero} \equiv \lambda x.x\mathbf{T}$$

since:

$$\begin{aligned} \mathbf{IT} \quad &= \mathbf{T} \\ [\mathbf{F}, n]\mathbf{T} &= \mathbf{F} \end{aligned}$$

Given this encoding and the two functions and the predicate, we can define more sophisticated functions such as addition:

$$+xy = \mathbf{if}(\mathbf{Zero}\ x)y(+(\mathbf{P}^-x)(\mathbf{S}^+y))$$

(use Proposition 6.5 from the end of the previous section).

This encoding for numerals is by no means the only possibility. Before introducing another encoding we make some definitions:

Definition 6.11 *A numeral system is a sequence:*

$$\mathbf{d} = d_0, d_1, \ldots$$

consisting of closed terms such that there are λ-terms, S_d^+ and $Zero_d$ such that:

$$\begin{aligned} S_d^+\ d_n \quad &= d_{n+1} \\ Zero_d\ d_0 \quad &= \mathbf{T} \\ Zero_d\ d_{n+1} &= \mathbf{F} \end{aligned}$$

for all numbers n, i.e. we have codes for all numerals, the successor func-
tion and a test for zero.

Definition 6.12 d *is a* normal *numeral system if each* d_n *has a normal form.*

Definition 6.13 $s = \ulcorner 0 \urcorner, \ulcorner 1 \urcorner, \ldots$ *with successor function* $\mathbf{S}^+$ *is called the* standard *numeral system.*

It is clear that the numerals in the standard numeral system are all distinct normal forms; thus the standard numeral system is a normal system.

   d is determined by d_0 and S_d^+, so we often write:

$$\mathbf{d} = (d_0, S^+)$$

A foretaste of the next section is given by the following definition:

Definition 6.14 *Let* **d** *be a numeral system, a numeric function:*

$$\phi : N^p \to N$$

(where N is the set of natural numbers) is λ-*definable with respect to* **d** *if:*

$$\exists F. \forall n_1, \ldots, n_p \in N. F d_{n_1} \ldots d_{n_p} = d_{\phi(n_1, \ldots, n_p)}$$

We say that **d** *is* adequate *if and only if all recursive functions are* λ-*definable with respect to* **d**. *Alternatively,* **d** *is adequate if and only if we can define a predecessor function for* **d**.

The alternative definition of adequacy is proved to be equivalent to the first definition at the end of the next section.

   An alternative encoding of the numerals is due to Church:

Definition 6.15 (Church Numerals) $c = c_0, c_1, \ldots$

$$c_n = \lambda f x . f^n(x)$$

The successor function is defined by:

$$S_c^+ c_n \equiv \lambda abc.b(abc)$$

Exercise 6.2.2 *Verify that* S_c^+ *is a suitable definition for the successor function.*

We can define translation functions between the standard and Church numerals, H and H^{-1}, such that:

$$H \ulcorner n \urcorner = c_n$$

and

$$H^{-1} c_n = \ulcorner n \urcorner$$

These functions are realised in the following way:

$$Hx \quad = \textbf{if } (\textbf{Zero } x) \; c_0 \; S_c^+(H(\mathbf{P}^- x))$$
$$H^{-1}c_n = c_n \; \mathbf{S}^+(\ulcorner 0 \urcorner)$$

Given these, we can define a test-for-zero:

$$Zero_c \equiv \textbf{Zero} \circ H^{-1}$$

The Church numeral system is also adequate, since we can define a predecessor function:

$$P_c^- \equiv H \circ \mathbf{P}^- \circ H^{-1}$$

The Church numerals are of interest because we can define some of the more powerful arithmetic functions without recursion.

Exercise 6.2.3 *What is $x \circ y$ for Church numerals x and y?*

6.3 λ-definability

We can specialise Definition 6.14 to the standard numeral system. In this case we talk about a numeric function being λ-definable (without specifying a numeral system). Since standard numerals are normal forms, in particular $\ulcorner \phi(n_1, \ldots, n_p) \urcorner$ is a normal form, we also have, by the Church–Rosser theorem, that:

$$F\ulcorner n_1 \urcorner \ldots \ulcorner n_p \urcorner \twoheadrightarrow \ulcorner \phi(n_1, \ldots, n_p) \urcorner$$

Our definition implicitly assumes that the given numeric function is total, i.e. defined on its whole domain. The results can be extended to partial functions but we will mainly consider total functions in this section; there is a brief discussion of partial functions at the end of the section. We start by defining the class of total recursive functions and then proceed to demonstrate that the functions in this class are all λ-definable.

Definition 6.16 (Initial Functions)
We define the following numeric functions to be the initial *functions:*

$$U_{i,p}(n_0, \ldots, n_p) = n_i \quad 0 \le i \le p$$
$$S^+(n) \qquad\qquad = n + 1$$
$$Z(n) \qquad\qquad = 0$$

i.e. a family of selector functions, a successor function and a constant zero function.

If $P(n)$ is a numeric relation, we use the notation:

$$\mu m[P(m)]$$

to denote the least number m for which $P(m)$ holds; or to denote undefined if there is no such m.

Given a class of numeric functions, A, we consider the following closure operators on the class:

Definition 6.17 A *is* closed under composition *if for all ϕ defined by:*

$$\phi(\vec{n}) = H(G_1(\vec{n}), \ldots, G_m(\vec{n}))$$

with $H, G_1, \ldots, G_m \in A$, one has $\phi \in A$.

A *is* closed under primitive recursion *if for all ϕ defined by:*

$$\phi(0, \vec{n}) \quad = H(\vec{n})$$
$$\phi(k+1, \vec{n}) = G(\phi(k, \vec{n}), k, \vec{n})$$

with $H, G \in A$, one has $\phi \in A$.

A *is* closed under minimalisation *if for all ϕ defined by:*

$$\phi(\vec{n}) = \mu m[H(\vec{n}, m) = 0]$$

with $H \in A$, such that[5]:

$$\forall \vec{n}.\exists m.H(\vec{n}, m) = 0$$

one has $\phi \in A$.

Notice that the primitive recursion construction is similar to the for-loop construction found in Algol-like languages; it provides iteration for a predetermined number of steps. It is possible to define most of the basic arithmetic functions using primitive recursion, for example:

$$plus(0, y) \quad = id(y)$$
$$plus(k+1, y) = F(plus(k, y), k, y)$$
$$\text{where } F(x, y, z) = S^+(U_{0,2}(x, y, z))$$

where id is the identity function. In contrast, the minimalisation construct corresponds to the more general form of iteration represented by `while...do...` and `repeat...until...` loops in Algol-like languages.

The class of *recursive* functions may now be defined formally as the least class of numeric functions which contains all of the initial functions and is closed under composition, primitive recursion and minimalisation.

We will now demonstrate that the initial functions are λ-definable and that the class of λ-definable functions is appropriately closed. First, we define:

$$U_{i,p} \equiv \lambda x_0 \ldots x_p.x_i$$
$$S^+ \equiv \lambda x.[\mathbf{F}, x]$$
$$Z \equiv \lambda x.\ulcorner 0 \urcorner$$

---

[5]This condition ensures that ϕ is total.

Now suppose that $H, G_1, \ldots, G_m$ are λ-defined by $S, T_1, \ldots, T_m$, then:

$$\phi(\vec{n}) = H(G_1(\vec{n}), \ldots, G_m(\vec{n}))$$

is λ-defined by:

$$F \equiv \lambda \vec{x}.S(T_1 \vec{x}) \ldots (T_m \vec{x})$$

If ϕ is defined by:

$$\begin{aligned} \phi(0, \vec{n}) &= H(\vec{n}) \\ \phi(k+1, \vec{n}) &= G(\phi(k, \vec{n}), k, \vec{n}) \end{aligned}$$

with H and G λ-defined by S and T respectively, then ϕ is λ-defined by:

$$F \equiv \mathbf{Y}\lambda fx\vec{y}.(Zero\ x)\ (S\vec{y})\ (T(f(\mathbf{P}^- x)\vec{y})(\mathbf{P}^- x)\vec{y})$$

In order to define minimalisation, we first define a function which, given a predicate λ-defined by P, determines the least numeral which satisfies P. We start by defining:

$$H_P \equiv \Theta(\lambda hz.(Pz)z(h(S^+ z)))$$

which just iterates from a given numeral, z, until (Pz) is true and returns z. The required function, written μP, is defined thus:

$$\mu P \equiv H_P \ulcorner 0 \urcorner$$

Then suppose that ϕ is defined by:

$$\phi(\vec{n}) = \mu m[H(\vec{n}, m) = 0]$$

where H is λ-defined by S; then ϕ is λ-defined by:

$$F \equiv \lambda \vec{x}.\mu[\lambda y.Zero(S\vec{x}y)]$$

From the preceding paragraphs, we have that the initial functions are λ-definable and that the three function-forming operations can be encoded in the λ-calculus. Consequently, we can infer that all (total) recursive functions are λ-definable. We also have the following result:

Theorem 6.18 *If ϕ is λ-defined by F, then $\forall \vec{n}, m \in N$:*

$$\phi(\vec{n}) = m \Leftrightarrow F \ulcorner \vec{n} \urcorner = \ulcorner m \urcorner$$

Proof
($\Rightarrow$) by definition
($\Leftarrow$)
Suppose $F \ulcorner \vec{n} \urcorner = \ulcorner m \urcorner$ then $\ulcorner \phi(\vec{n}) \urcorner = \ulcorner m \urcorner$. Since numerals are distinct normal forms, it follows from the Church–Rosser theorem that $\phi(\vec{n}) = m$.
$\square$

Putting these two results together, we get the following theorem (due to Kleene):

Theorem 6.19 *The λ-definable numeric functions are exactly the recursive functions.*

We now return to the question of adequacy of a numeral system.

Proposition 6.20 d *is adequate* $\Leftrightarrow \exists P_d^- . \forall n \in N . P_d^- \; d_{n+1} = d_n$.

Proof
($\Rightarrow$) follows from the definition of adequacy since predecessor is a recursive function.

($\Leftarrow$) if, in addition to successor and test-for-zero, **d** is equipped with a predecessor function then it can be shown that the class of recursive functions are λ-definable with respect to **d** by using the foregoing results, replacing the standard numeral system by **d**.   □

Finally, the definition can be extended to partial functions in the following way:

Definition 6.21 *A partial numeric function, ϕ, with p arguments is λ-definable if for some $F \in \Lambda$:*
$\forall \vec{n} \in N^p$.

$$F \ulcorner \vec{n} \urcorner = \ulcorner \phi(\vec{n}) \urcorner \; if \; \phi(\vec{n}) \; converges \; (i.e. \; is \; defined)$$
$$F \ulcorner \vec{n} \urcorner \; without \; hnf \; otherwise$$

where $\vec{n} \equiv n_1, \ldots, n_p$

In this section we have characterised the class of functions which are λ-definable. In general, the link between λ-definability and Recursive Function Theory is:

$$\phi \; is \; \lambda\text{-definable} \Leftrightarrow \phi \; is \; partial \; recursive$$

Given another result from Computability Theory:

$$\phi \; is \; partial \; recursive \Leftrightarrow \phi \; is \; Turing \; Computable$$

we see that λ-definability, according to the Church–Turing thesis, can be claimed to capture the notion of *effective calculability*.

6.4   Decidability

One of the fundamental theorems of Mathematical Logic is Gödel's Incompleteness Theorem; the details of the theorem are tangential to this book but the proof of the theorem uses a coding technique which gives an effective way of associating a unique integer, the Gödel number, with each sentence in some theory. Translating this result to the λ-calculus, we have that there is an algorithmic injective map $\# : \Lambda \to N$ such that $\#M$ is the Gödel number of M. Using this notion, we can state the Second Fixed Point Theorem:

Theorem 6.22 (The Second Fixed Point Theorem)

$$\forall F.\exists X.F^\ulcorner \#X^\urcorner = X$$

Proof
Define:

$$\mathbf{Ap}^\ulcorner \#M^\urcorner(^\ulcorner \#N^\urcorner) = {}^\ulcorner \#(MN)^\urcorner$$
$$\mathbf{Num}^\ulcorner \#n^\urcorner \qquad = {}^\ulcorner \#(^\ulcorner \#n^\urcorner)^\urcorner$$

Now take $W \equiv \lambda x.F(\mathbf{Ap}\ x(\mathbf{Num}\ x))$ and $X \equiv W^\ulcorner \#W^\urcorner$; then:

$$
\begin{aligned}
X &\to F(\mathbf{Ap}^\ulcorner \#W^\urcorner(\mathbf{Num}^\ulcorner \#W^\urcorner)) \\
&= F(\mathbf{Ap}^\ulcorner \#W^\urcorner(^\ulcorner \#^\ulcorner \#W^\urcorner{}^\urcorner)) \\
&= F(^\ulcorner \#(W^\ulcorner \#W^\urcorner)^\urcorner) \\
&\equiv F^\ulcorner \#X^\urcorner \text{ as required}
\end{aligned}
$$

$\square$

Notice how this construction parallels the proof of the Fixed Point Theorem. Its importance for us is that it allows us to prove Scott's Theorem (the analogue of Rice's Theorem — see Hopcroft and Ullman's book) and thereby answer some important questions about decidability in the λ-calculus.

First, we need some definitions; in the following we assume that A and B are subsets of λ-terms:

Definition 6.23 *A is* non-trivial *if $A \neq \emptyset$ and $A \neq \Lambda$.*

Definition 6.24 *A is* closed under equality *if:*

$$\forall M, N \in \Lambda[M \in A \wedge M = N \Rightarrow N \in A]$$

Definition 6.25 *A and B are* recursively separable *iff there is a recursive set[6] C such that:*

$$(A \subseteq C) \wedge (B \cap C = \emptyset)$$

Scott's Theorem may be stated thus:

Theorem 6.26 (Scott's Theorem)
(i) Let A and B, subsets of Λ, be non-empty sets closed under equality. Then A and B are not recursively separable.
(ii) Let A, a subset of Λ, be a non-trivial set closed under equality. Then A is not recursive.

---

[6] By the term "recursive set" we mean a set whose membership predicate is recursive; i.e. there is a Turing machine which for any potential element either halts with an indication that the element is a member or halts with a contrary indication.

Proof

(i) Let $M_0 \in A$ and $M_1 \in B$ and C be a recursive set which separates A and B. The characteristic function (i.e. membership predicate) of $\#C^7$ is recursive and defined by F. Hence:

$$M \in C \Rightarrow F^\ulcorner \#M^\urcorner = {}^\ulcorner 0^\urcorner$$
$$M \notin C \Rightarrow F^\ulcorner \#M^\urcorner = {}^\ulcorner 1^\urcorner$$

Define:

$$G \equiv \lambda x.(Zero(Fx))M_1 M_0$$

then:

$$M \in C \Rightarrow G^\ulcorner \#M^\urcorner = M_1$$
$$M \notin C \Rightarrow G^\ulcorner \#M^\urcorner = M_0$$

but, by the Second Fixed Point Theorem:

$$G^\ulcorner \#X^\urcorner = X \text{ for some } X$$

and so:

$$X \in C \Rightarrow X = G^\ulcorner \#X^\urcorner = M_1 \in B \Rightarrow X \notin C$$
$$X \notin C \Rightarrow X = G^\ulcorner \#X^\urcorner = M_0 \in A \Rightarrow X \in C$$

Contradiction!

(ii) If A is a non-trivial set closed under equality, then (i) applies to A and its complement. Hence A cannot be recursive. □

As a consequence of Scott's theorem there are two further theorems that can be proved. The first concerns the undecidability of the question as to whether an arbitrary term has a normal form — this is equivalent, in some senses, to the Halting Problem for Turing Machines. The theorem is formally stated:

Theorem 6.27 $\{M \mid M \text{ has a nf}\}$ *is an recursively enumerable*[8] *set which is not recursive.*

Proof
The set is r.e. since:

$$M \text{ has a nf} \Leftrightarrow \exists N.N \text{ is an nf and } \lambda \vdash M = N$$

---

[7]If A is a subset of Λ then:

$$\#A = \{\#M \mid M \in A\}$$

[8]A set is *recursively enumerable* if we can construct a Turing machine which, given a potential element, will stop with the answer YES if the element is in the set but may not halt otherwise.

i.e. we can construct a procedure which tests M for equality against a sequence of normal forms; if the procedure halts, M has a normal form but, since there are an infinite number of normal forms, the procedure may not halt.

But M is non-trivial ($\lambda x.x \in M$ so $M \neq \emptyset$ and $\Omega \notin M$ so $M \neq \Lambda$) and closed under equality and therefore by Scott's Theorem (ii) M is not recursive. $\qquad\square$

The second theorem concerns the undecidability of λ. First we define the notion of *essential undecidability*:

Definition 6.28 *A theory $\mathcal{T}$ is essentially undecidable iff $\mathcal{T}$ is consistent and has no consistent recursive extension.*

The theorem is then:

Theorem 6.29 λ *is essentially undecidable*

Proof
Let $\mathcal{T}$ be a consistent extension of λ, then let $X = \{M \mid \mathcal{T} \vdash M = \mathbf{I}\}$.
X is not empty because surely $\mathcal{T} \vdash \mathbf{I} = \mathbf{I}$!
$X \neq \Lambda$ because $\mathcal{T}$ is consistent.
X is clearly closed under equality.
Thus, by Scott's Theorem (ii), X is not recursive and thus $\mathcal{T}$ is not recursive. $\qquad\square$

6.5 Summary

In this chapter we have revisited the concept of fixed point combinators and have seen that there is an infinite variety of such combinators. We have the existence of such combinators in the construction of encodings for numerals and numeric functions, leading to the important concept of λ-definability. Based on this work, we were able to show the equivalence of λ-definable functions and Recursive Functions (and indirectly Turing computable functions). We closed with Scott's theorem and two important decidability results for the λ-calculus.

7

Types

Overview

The type-free λ-calculus has been presented as a prototypical functional programming language. While it is true that many of the issues that we have studied have direct relevance to programming practice, the theory fails to match the practice in a number of important ways. The majority of modern functional programming languages are typed. As a consequence, we can no longer construct certain terms which play a key part in the foregoing theory. In this chapter we present three typed calculi. First we consider the simply typed λ-calculus; this calculus is derived from the type-free λ-calculus in a fairly direct way but has a rather different character as a result of the typing. For example β-reduction in the typed λ-calculus is strongly normalising.

Most modern functional languages are typed but allow the definition of polymorphic functions. We introduce the second-order polymorphic λ-calculus. This provides a theoretical account of a slightly more powerful type system than is usually provided for functional languages. The Hindley–Milner type system, which is the basis for the type systems used in functional languages, is discussed in Chapter 8.

Finally, we present the notion of intersection types. These were originally introduced by Barendregt, Coppo and Dezani to construct a λ model. From a practical point of view, intersection types may be used to give an account of *overloading*. More recently, intersection types have played a role in program analysis, for example strictness analysis (an alternative approach is discussed in Chapter 8).

7.1 Typed λ-calculus

We start our study of typed calculi with the simply typed λ-calculus; this calculus has a strong typing discipline similar to that adopted in PASCAL and other typed imperative languages — each term has a single (monomorphic) type associated with it. The simply typed λ-calculus is in many ways simpler than the (type-free) λ-calculus; for example self-application, which has been at the root of many of the problems we have encountered, is outlawed and thus all terms are strongly normalising and there are no fixed point combinators. Once again, in introducing a new calculus, we should address all of the issues that we have considered for the λ-calculus (reduction, models, computability, etc. . .) but instead we will just present the highlights.

There are two approaches that can be taken in defining a typed calculus. The first, originated by Curry, is called *implicit* typing; the terms are the same as the type-free calculus and each term has a set of possible types assigned to it. The second approach, originated by Church, is called *explicit* typing; terms are annotated with type information which uniquely determines a type for the term. In the following, we will follow Church's approach.

Since terms will have types associated with them, we start by considering the syntax of types:

Definition 7.1 (Types)
The set of types, Typ, is the least set such that:

(1) $0 \in Typ$
(2) *if $\sigma, \tau \in Typ$ then $(\sigma \to \tau) \in Typ$*

The type 0 is a *ground* type. Notice that we only have a single ground type; later we will see that it plays the role of a type variable. In a more realistic language, we might differentiate between type constants and variables; for example in a programming language context, the type constants are the "built-in" types such as integers, booleans and characters. However, since we are considering a pure calculus it is sufficient to restrict ourselves to a single ground type. Types of the form $(\sigma \to \tau)$ correspond to a function type; a function of this type takes arguments of type σ and returns a result of type τ. Examples of types are:

$$0 \qquad (0 \to 0) \qquad ((0 \to 0) \to (0 \to 0))$$

If we adopt the convention that $\to$ associates to the right[1], we can omit the majority of the parentheses:

$$0 \qquad 0 \to 0 \qquad (0 \to 0) \to 0 \to 0$$

Terms in the typed λ-calculus are words over the alphabet:

$v_0^\sigma, v_1^\sigma, \ldots$ variables, a distinct set for each $\sigma \in Typ$
λ
$(,)$ parentheses

The class of typed λ-terms is written Λ^τ; when we want to talk about the class of terms of some specific type, σ, we write Λ_σ.

---

[1] A moment's thought should convince the reader that this convention is consistent with the left associativity of application.

Definition 7.2 (Typed Terms)
The class Λ^τ is the class:

$$\bigcup\{\Lambda_\sigma \mid \sigma \in Typ\}$$

and the Λ_σ are such that:

(1) $v_i^\sigma \in \Lambda_\sigma$
(2) $M \in \Lambda_{\sigma\to\tau}, N \in \Lambda_\sigma \Rightarrow (MN) \in \Lambda_\tau$
(3) $M \in \Lambda_\tau, x \in \Lambda_\sigma \Rightarrow (\lambda x.M) \in \Lambda_{\sigma\to\tau}$

Free/bound variables, closed terms and substitution are defined in the obvious way (by analogy to the type-free calculus). Care must be taken to respect the types; for example:

$$FV(\lambda v^0.v^{0\to 0}) = \{v^{0\to 0}\}$$

The theories λ^τ and $\lambda\eta^{\tau\,2}$ are defined in the same way as the corresponding type-free theories but the types of terms have to make sense, for example:

$$(\lambda x^\sigma.M)N = M[x^\sigma := N] \text{ if } N \in \Lambda_\sigma$$

and formulae are of the form:

$$M = N \text{ with } M, N \in \Lambda_\sigma \text{ for arbitrary type } \sigma$$

We could equally well embark on a study of typed Combinatory Logic; there we would need to introduce a class of combinators in place of each of the type-free combinators **S** and **K**:

$$\mathbf{K}_{\sigma\tau} \in \mathcal{C}_{\sigma\to\tau\to\sigma}$$
$$\mathbf{S}_{\sigma\tau\rho} \in \mathcal{C}_{(\sigma\to\tau\to\rho)\to((\sigma\to\tau)\to\sigma\to\rho)}$$

It is worth considering how the type of $\mathbf{S}_{\sigma\tau\rho}$ is justified:

- Recall that $\mathbf{S}ABC = AC(BC)$
- Suppose that the type of $\mathbf{S}ABC$ is ρ
- Then $AC(BC) \in \mathcal{C}_\rho$
- Suppose that $C \in \mathcal{C}_\sigma$ and $(BC) \in \mathcal{C}_\tau$
- Then $A \in \mathcal{C}_{\sigma\to\tau\to\rho}$ and $B \in \mathcal{C}_{\sigma\to\tau}$ which gives the overall type of $\mathbf{S}_{\sigma\tau\rho}$

Notions of reduction in the typed λ-calculus are the obvious analogues of the notions that we introduced in the type-free case:

$$\beta = \{(((\lambda x^\sigma.M)N), M[x^\sigma := N]) \mid M \in \Lambda_\tau, N \in \Lambda_\sigma \text{ for some } \sigma, \tau \in Typ\}$$

$$\eta = \{(((\lambda x^\sigma.Mx^\sigma), M) \mid M \in \Lambda_{\sigma\to\tau} \text{ for some } \sigma, \tau \in Typ, x^\sigma \notin (FVM)\}$$

By analogy with the type-free case we have that $\beta(\eta)$ is CR.

---

[2]In future we will write $\lambda(\eta)^\tau$ to stand for either of these theories.

Strong Normalisation

An essential difference between the type-free and the typed calculus is that, in the latter case, $\beta(\eta)$ is strongly normalising (SN), i.e. $\beta\eta\text{-}SN$. In this subsection we present a proof of this result; the proof was discovered by Tait in 1967 and our account is based on that of Hindley and Seldin.

We start with a definition:

Definition 7.3 (Strong Computability — SC)

(1) $\forall M \in \Lambda_0[SC(M) \Leftrightarrow SN(M)]$

(2) $\forall M \in \Lambda_{\sigma \to \tau}[SC(M) \Leftrightarrow \forall N \in \Lambda_\sigma[SC(N) \ implies \ SC(MN)]]$

The proof of the strong normalisation result follows in two steps by firstly showing that every strongly computable term is also strongly normalising and secondly showing that every typed term is strongly computable. We start with some observations:

• Every type σ can be written in a unique way in the form:

$$\sigma_1 \to \ldots \to \sigma_n \to 0$$

• If $M \in \Lambda_\sigma$ is strongly normalising then so is every subterm of M.

The first follows from the definition of types, the second follows because if a subterm of M is not strongly normalising then the same infinite reduction is possible for the whole term.

We start by showing that every strongly computable term is strongly normalising. The proof uses a new form of induction: induction over the structure of types.

Lemma 7.4 *Let σ be any type:*

(1) *Every term $(vM_1 \ldots M_n) \in \Lambda_\sigma$, where $M_1, \ldots, M_n$ are all strongly normalising, is strongly computable.*

(2) *Every strongly computable term of type σ is strongly normalising.*

Proof

• $\sigma \equiv 0$: both properties follow from the definitions.
• $\sigma \equiv \alpha \to \beta$:
  (1) Let $N \in \Lambda_\alpha$ such that $SC(N)$. By the IH(2), $SN(N)$. Then by IH(1), $SC(vM_1 \ldots M_n N)$ and thus $SC(vM_1 \ldots M_n)$ by definition.

  (2) Let $N \in \Lambda_\sigma$ such that $SC(N)$ and let v^α not occur (at all) in N. By IH(1), $SC(v^\alpha)$ (set $n = 0$). Hence $SC(Nv)$ and by IH(2) $SN(Nv)$; but then, by our second observation, we have $SN(N)$.

□

To show that all terms are strongly computable, we need an intermediate result that if the contractum of a redex and any terms erased by the redex are strongly computable then the redex is as well.

Lemma 7.5 *If $SC(M[x^\alpha := N])$ then, provided that $SC(N)$ if x^α is not free in M, $SC((\lambda x^\alpha.M)N)$.*

Proof
Suppose $M \in \Lambda_\tau$ and let $\tau = \tau_1 \to \ldots \to \tau_n \to 0$ and let $M_i \in \Lambda_{\tau_i}$ be such that $SC(M_i)$ for $1 \le i \le n$. Then

$$SN(M[x := N]M_1 \ldots M_n)$$

but then we have

$$SN((\lambda x.M)NM_1 \ldots M_n)$$

since any infinite reduction from the latter term can also be "reached" from the former. Thus

$$SC((\lambda x.M)NM_1 \ldots M_n)$$

and $SC((\lambda x.M)N)$. $\qquad\qquad\qquad\qquad\qquad\qquad\qquad\qquad\qquad\quad$ $\square$

We now prove that every term is strongly computable; since we have proved that all strongly computable terms are strongly normalisable we will be done. As is often the case it is easier to prove a slightly stronger result.

Theorem 7.6 *For every term $M \in \Lambda_\sigma$, for all $x_1^{\alpha_1}, \ldots, x_n^{\alpha_n}$ and N_i such that $SC(N_i)$ ($1 \le i \le n$), the term $M^* \equiv M[x_1 := N_1] \ldots [x_n := N_n]$ is strongly computable.*

Proof
(induction over the structure of M)

- $M \equiv x_i$: trivial.
- M a variable, distinct from the x_i: follows by Lemma 7.4.
- $M \equiv PQ$: then $M^* \equiv P^*Q^*$ and by the IH $SC(P^*)$ and $SC(Q^*)$. Thus $SC(M^*)$ follows from the definition.
- $M \equiv \lambda x^\gamma.P$ and $\sigma \equiv (\gamma \to \delta)$: then $M^* \equiv \lambda x.P^*$. Suppose that $N \in \Lambda_\gamma$ and $SC(N)$, then $M^*N \to P^*[x := N]$. Now $SC(P^*[x := N])$ follows from the IH and thus, by Lemma 7.5, $SC(M^*N)$. $SC(M^*)$ follows from the definition.

$\qquad\qquad\qquad\qquad\qquad\qquad\qquad\qquad\qquad\qquad\qquad\qquad\qquad\qquad$ $\square$

If we choose each N_i to be x_i (which is strongly computable by Lemma 7.4), we get that every term is strongly computable.

Exercise 7.1.1 *Show that $\beta\eta$ is WCR in $\lambda\eta^\tau$ and hence deduce that $\beta\eta$ is CR.*

As a consequence of the strong normalisation result, all typed terms have normal forms; moreover, provable equality in $\lambda(\eta)^\tau$ is decidable:

Proposition 7.7 $\lambda(\eta)^\tau \vdash M = N$ *implies M and N have the same $\beta(\eta)$-nfs.*
The nfs can be found effectively by SN.

It should be fairly obvious that many type-free terms can be given a type (or many types!). For example:

$$\lambda x.x$$

can be typed as:

$$\lambda x^\sigma.x^\sigma \in \Lambda_{\sigma\to\sigma} \text{ for all } \sigma \in Typ$$

that is: "$\sigma \to \sigma$ is a possible type for $\lambda x.x \in \Lambda$". However, there are many terms that can not be assigned a type; given our earlier comments and the structure of the typed terms, it should be clear that any term involving self-application falls into this category, for example:

- In order to assign a type to $\lambda x.xx$, we must assign a type to xx.
- In order to assign a type to xx, x must have type $\alpha \to \beta$ <u>and</u> type α.

Suppose $M \in \Lambda_\sigma$, we write $\mid M \mid (\in \Lambda)$ for the term produced by erasing all of the type symbols in M; clearly, $\mid M \mid$ is typable and a possible type is σ. If σ is a type then σ^* is an instance of σ if it results from σ by replacing some of the 0's in σ by some other type:

Example 7.8 *Some instances of 0:*

$$0 \to 0, \qquad 0 \to 0 \to 0, \qquad ((0 \to 0 \to 0) \to (0 \to 0) \to 0 \to 0)$$

Some instances of $0 \to 0$:

$$(0 \to 0) \to 0 \to 0, \qquad (0 \to 0 \to 0) \to 0 \to 0 \to 0$$

Exercise 7.1.2 *Write down some terms with the above types.*

Two important results concerning these issues were first discovered by Roger Hindley; we state them without proof:

Proposition 7.9

(1) *The set of typable λ-terms is recursive; i.e. there is an algorithm which will decide whether a given term is typable or not.*

(2) *If $M \in \Lambda$ is typable then one can find a unique $\sigma \in Typ$ such that every possible type for M is an instance of σ; σ is called the* principal type scheme *for M.*

We will return to this in the next chapter.

Since we cannot have fixed point combinators in the typed λ-calculus, the reader may have wondered about the impact this has on computability. We can define a notion of λ^τ-definability analogously to λ-definability but there are some problems. The first problem is that we cannot use the standard numerals:

$$\ulcorner 0 \urcorner \quad \equiv \mathbf{I}$$
$$\ulcorner n+1 \urcorner \equiv [\mathbf{F}, \ulcorner n \urcorner]$$

since the numerals all have different types, for example:

$$\ulcorner 0 \urcorner \equiv \mathbf{I} \qquad \text{has type } 0 \to 0$$
$$\ulcorner 1 \urcorner \equiv \lambda z.z\mathbf{FI} \text{ has type } ((0 \to 0 \to 0) \to (0 \to 0) \to 0) \to 0$$

As a consequence, the successor function (for example) is untypable! However, the Church numerals all have the same type:

$$c_n \equiv \lambda fx.f^n x$$

$$c_n \in \Lambda_{(0 \to 0) \to 0 \to 0}$$

Definition 7.10 *The* extended polynomials *are the least class of numeric functions containing:*

(1) *Projections: $U_{i,n}$*
(2) *Constant functions*
(3) *The sg function : $sg \ 0 = 0$, $sg \ (n+1) = 1$*

and is closed under addition and multiplication.

It turns out that it is exactly this class of functions which is λ^τ-definable on the Church numerals; the interested reader is referred to the literature for the proof. Using constant functions, addition and multiplication it is possible to construct functions which have polynomial expressions as bodies. The adjective "extended" is used in the definition to indicate that we can encode conditional functions using the *sg* function (with multiplication).

We close this section by considering three uses of the typed λ-calculus, the latter two being of more relevance to Computer Science. We briefly sketch the applications and, once again, encourage the interested reader to refer to the literature.

Consistency of Arithmetic

The first application we identify is in the proof of the consistency of arithmetic. The proof is due to Gödel; he worked with an extended theory, $\mathfrak{I}$, which contains the new constants:

$$0 \quad \in \Lambda\mathfrak{I}_0$$
$$S^+ \in \Lambda\mathfrak{I}_{0 \to 0}$$
$$R_\sigma \in \Lambda_{\sigma \to (\sigma \to 0 \to \sigma) \to 0 \to \sigma}$$

The final "constant" represents a class of typed recursion operators, axiomatised in the following way:

$$R_\sigma M N 0 \quad\ = M$$
$$R_\sigma M N(S^+ x) = N(R_\sigma M N x)x$$

There are appropriate notions of $\beta\mathfrak{I}$- and $\beta\eta\mathfrak{I}$-reduction on $\Lambda\mathfrak{I}$ which have been shown to be CR. Notice that the recursion operators effectively encode primitive recursion and consequently it should not surprise the reader that $\beta\eta\mathfrak{I}$-reduction is SN.

There have been a number of extensions to Gödel's $\mathfrak{I}$. For example, Spector proved the consistency of analysis by extending $\mathfrak{I}$ with a new recursion operator called *bar recursion*.

Logic of Computable Functions

The phrase *Logic of Computable Functions* originated with Scott. The system LCF, developed by Milner, Gordon and Wadsworth, is a semi-automatic theorem prover which is used to prove properties of programs. The system has two parts: a meta-language which is used to describe proof tactics[3] and an object language, $PP\lambda$, in which proofs are written. $PP\lambda$ is similar to $\mathfrak{I}$ with the following extensions:

(1) There are more types:

$\sigma \times \tau$	the direct product
	allowing the construction of pairs
$\sigma \oplus \tau$	the disjoint sum
	allowing the definition of algebraic data types

(2) For each σ, there is a fixed point combinator[4]:

$$\mathbf{Y}_\sigma : (\sigma \to \sigma) \to \sigma$$

$$\mathbf{Y}_\sigma M = M(\mathbf{Y}_\sigma M)$$

---

[3]This is the language ML which has become an extremely successful programming language. ML has a polymorphic type system — a subject which we shall study in the next chapter.

[4]Consequently reduction in $PP\lambda$ is not SN.

(3) The theory is embedded in predicate logic.

Formulae as Types — The Curry–Howard Isomorphism

The astute reader may have noticed that there is a similarity between the rules for types and the rules for propositional logic. For example, the rule for application:

$$\frac{\alpha \quad \alpha \to \beta}{\beta}$$

is the rule Modus Ponens; there are similar relationships between $\times$ and conjunction and $\oplus$ and disjunction. Reduction of terms with the types above the line produces a term with the type below the line; thus this "program" and its execution constitute a proof of the rule. This association between proofs and programs is known as the Curry–Howard isomorphism. The theorem proving system Automath (see our discussion of de Bruijn notation in Chapter 2) uses this technique.

7.2   The Polymorphic λ-calculus

This calculus was invented independently by Girard (1972 — his interest was in extending the Curry–Howard isomorphism — see above — to include quantification) and Reynolds (1974 — his interest was in programming language theory). Just as the λ-calculus and functional programming have been sloganised by "functions as first class citizens" (Stoy), the 2nd-order λ-calculus can be sloganised by "Types as first class citizens"; types can be abstracted just as normal values:

Example 7.11 (A polymorphic identity function:)

$$M \equiv \Lambda t.\lambda x \in t.x$$

we can then specialise this term to a particular type by application:

$$M int \text{ or } M[int]$$

Type schemes in this calculus are constructed in the following way:

$$\sigma ::= \alpha \mid \iota \mid \sigma_1 \to \sigma_2 \mid \forall \alpha.\sigma$$

where α is a type variable and ι is a type constant. The last component is the type scheme associated with Λ-abstractions.

Definition 7.12 *The terms of the 2nd-order polymorphic λ-calculus, Λ_2, are the least class such that:*

(1) *Every variable and constant is in Λ_2.*

(2) *$M, N \in \Lambda_2 \Rightarrow (MN) \in \Lambda_2$.*

(3) *$M \in \Lambda_2$, x a variable, σ a type scheme $\Rightarrow (\lambda x \in \sigma.M) \in \Lambda_2$.*

(4) *$M \in \Lambda_2$, σ a type scheme $\Rightarrow (M\sigma) \in \Lambda_2$.*

(5) $M \in \Lambda_2$, α *a type variable* $\Rightarrow (\Lambda\alpha.M) \in \Lambda_2$.

Substitution and α-congruence are defined in the obvious way. We have two β-conversion axioms:

$$
\begin{array}{lll}
(\beta^1) & (\lambda x \in \sigma.M)N = M[x := N] \\
(\beta^2) & (\Lambda t.M)\sigma \quad = M[t := \sigma]
\end{array}
$$

Of course it is also possible to define η-conversion. Some basic facts concerning $\beta\eta$-reduction are:

- $\beta\eta$ is CR
- Every Λ_2 term has a $\beta\eta$-nf
- $\beta\eta$ is SN

We now present a formal system for type inference in the 2nd-order polymorphic λ-calculus. Basic judgements have the following form:

$$A \vdash e : \sigma$$

where A is a list of assumptions of the form $x : \sigma$. The axioms and rules are:

$$A \vdash x : \sigma \qquad\qquad (x : \sigma \text{ in } A)$$

$$\frac{A_x \cup \{x : \sigma\} \vdash M : \tau}{A \vdash (\lambda x \in \sigma.M) : \sigma \to \tau}$$

$$\frac{A \vdash M : \sigma \to \tau \quad A \vdash N : \sigma}{A \vdash (MN) : \tau}$$

$$\frac{A \vdash M : \sigma}{A \vdash (\Lambda t.M) : \forall t.\sigma} \qquad t \notin FV(A)$$

$$\frac{A \vdash M : \forall t.\sigma}{A \vdash (M\tau) : [\tau/t]\sigma}$$

where A_x is the same as A except any assumption about x has been removed.

For example, we have:

$$\frac{\dfrac{x : \alpha \vdash x : \alpha}{\vdash (\lambda x \in \alpha.x) : \alpha \to \alpha}}{\vdash (\Lambda\alpha\lambda x \in \alpha.x) : (\forall\alpha.\alpha \to \alpha)}$$

Exercise 7.2.1 *Construct a proof for the following judgement:*

$$\vdash (\Lambda\alpha\Lambda\beta\lambda x \in \alpha\lambda y \in \beta.x) : (\forall\alpha.\forall\beta.\alpha \to \beta \to \alpha)$$

In contrast to the simply typed λ-calculus of the last section, it is currently an open problem whether there is an algorithm for type checking or type inference in the second-order polymorphic λ-calculus.

Reynolds used the second-order polymorphic λ-calculus to model various programming language concepts such as type definitions, abstract data types and polymorphism.

The style of polymorphism found in most functional programming languages (discussed in Chapter 8) is a restricted version of that discussed above. In particular, the syntax of types in Λ_2 allows arbitrary nesting of quantifiers. For example, the following is a valid type in Λ_2:

$$\forall \alpha.(\forall \beta.\alpha \to \beta) \to \alpha \to \alpha$$

The type schemes assigned to terms in functional programming systems are usually *shallow*; the quantifiers are usually omitted and are implicitly at the outermost level. Consequently, the scope of all quantifiers is the whole scheme (to the right of the quantifier). The pay-off is that we regain the ability to define an algorithm for type inference.

7.3   Intersection Types

In the polymorphic λ-calculus a function can be applied to arguments of different types but the types of the arguments must have the same "structure". This becomes more apparent in the context of programming languages where we have a richer set of type constructors. For example, the standard *map* function found in many functional programming languages is polymorphic in its second argument but the argument must at least be a list structure. Most programming languages also allow overloading of operators, for example + can be applied to a pair of integers or a pair of reals — the operation performed in each case is very different. In terms involving overloaded operators functions are applied to arguments with structurally different types.

An *intersection* type is like a type in the simply typed calculus except types can be constructed using the intersection operator ∩ — a term which is assigned such a type has both types involved in the intersection. An example of how this is used is in the term $\lambda x.xx$, which is untypable in the previous two calculi, but we can show:

$$(\lambda x.xx) : (\sigma \cap (\sigma \to \tau)) \to \tau$$

Notice that the argument is given both σ and $\sigma \to \tau$ as types and thus the self-application in the body can be typed. In this section, we will present the $\lambda\cap$-calculus. In this calculus, it no longer makes sense to have explicit typing so we present an implicitly typed calculus.

The set of types is defined as follows:

$$\tau ::= \alpha \mid \iota \mid \tau \to \tau \mid \tau \cap \tau$$

Amongst the constants, we include a distinguished type ω.

The rôle of ω is as a *universal* type; any term can be assigned ω as a type. Given ω and $\cap$ it is fairly natural to order the types; we define the following pre-order:

$$\sigma \leq \sigma$$

$$\sigma \leq \omega \qquad \omega \leq \omega \to \omega$$

$$\sigma \cap \tau \leq \sigma \qquad \sigma \cap \tau \leq \tau$$

$$\frac{\sigma \leq \tau \quad \tau \leq \rho}{\sigma \leq \rho} \qquad \frac{\sigma \leq \tau \quad \sigma \leq \rho}{\sigma \leq \tau \cap \rho}$$

$$(\sigma \to \rho) \cap (\sigma \to \tau) \leq \sigma \to (\rho \cap \tau)$$

$$\frac{\sigma' \leq \sigma \quad \tau \leq \tau'}{(\sigma \to \tau) \leq (\sigma' \to \tau')}$$

We write $\sigma \equiv \tau$ in the case that $\sigma \leq \tau$ and $\tau \leq \sigma$. We also adopt the convention that $\cap$ has higher precedence than $\to$ which allows us to omit some parentheses.

Exercise 7.3.1 *Show that:*

$$(\sigma \cap \sigma' \to \tau) \equiv ((\sigma \to \tau) \cap (\sigma' \to \tau))$$

The last rule in the definition of $\leq$ expresses the fact that $\to$ is *contravariant* in its first argument.

The following inference system assigns intersection types to terms.

Taut $A \vdash x : \sigma$ $\qquad\qquad\qquad\qquad\qquad (x : \sigma) \in A$

Top $A \vdash M : \omega$

$$\to\text{E} \quad \frac{A \vdash M : (\sigma \to \tau) \quad A \vdash N : \sigma}{A \vdash M\,N : \tau} \qquad \to\text{I} \quad \frac{A_x \cup (x : \sigma) \vdash M : \tau}{A \vdash \lambda x.M : \sigma \to \tau}$$

$$\cap\text{E} \quad \frac{A \vdash M : (\sigma_1 \cap \sigma_2)}{A \vdash M : \sigma_i} \; i = 1, 2 \quad \cap\text{I} \quad \frac{A \vdash M : \sigma \quad A \vdash M : \tau}{A \vdash M : \sigma \cap \tau}$$

$$\text{Sub} \quad \frac{A \vdash M : \sigma \quad \sigma \leq \tau}{A \vdash M : \tau}$$

Exercise 7.3.2 *Infer two different types for $\lambda x.xx$ using the above system.*

In $\lambda\cap$, the following properties hold:

- $\beta\eta$ is CR.
- SN fails – every term from Λ is typable, including Ω; all terms have type ω.
- it is undecidable whether a term has a particular type.

van Bakel has studied a restricted inference system which does not have the **Top** rule; in this system, the following is true:

$$SN(M) \Leftrightarrow \exists A.\exists\sigma.A \vdash M : \sigma$$

Barendregt *et al* prove that:

M has a normal form $\Leftrightarrow \exists A.\exists\sigma.A \vdash M : \sigma$ and ω does not occur in σ

7.4 Summary

In this chapter we have seen a variety of typed calculi. We have discussed a simply typed monomorphic calculus and then seen how to introduce polymorphic terms. A common feature of the first two typed calculi that we have studied is that $(\beta\eta\text{-})$reduction is strongly normalising. For the third system, involving intersection types, SN fails; all terms can be typed and decidability fails.

8

Practical Issues

Overview

In this chapter we turn to more practical aspects of the λ-calculus.

One form of standard reduction sequence (see Chapter 3) is a leftmost sequence (reduce the leftmost redex at each stage); this is also called *normal order reduction*. Lazy evaluation systems use this reduction order (see later). A redex is *outermost* if it is not contained in any other redex, it is *innermost* if it does not contain any redexes. An alternative reduction strategy, called *applicative* order, is leftmost innermost. The features of the various evaluation strategies have been sloganised by Mycroft in terms of the way in which parameters are treated:

Normal Order: Evaluate arguments as often as they are used.

Applicative Order: Evaluate arguments once.

Lazy Evaluation: Evaluate arguments at most once.

From a pragmatic point of view applicative order is preferable to lazy evaluation (or normal order) since there is less run-time overhead and there is greater potential for parallel evaluation (since we know that the parameters will be evaluated we can go ahead and evaluate them in parallel with the function call). Lazy evaluation gains because if an argument is not used then it will not be evaluated; thus:

$$(\lambda xy.y)((\lambda x.xx)(\lambda x.xx))z$$

evaluates to its nf, z, whereas an applicative order reduction repeatedly tries to evaluate the Ω argument (to no avail!). It is usual to associate these evaluation orders with particular parameter passing mechanisms: call-by-name, call-by-value and call-by-need respectively. However, these associations are only approximate in the functional language setting. Normal order and applicative order both refer to reduction sequences that terminate in normal form. We have already observed that lazy functional systems stop some way short of normal forms (i.e. with weak head normal forms) but even strict functional systems (such as Standard ML) do not evaluate under λs. Strict functional systems compute weak normal forms ; a more detailed discussion of this point can be found in Reade's book. The result is that redexes in abstraction terms may be copied and therefore evaluated more than once in a strict functional language.

We will start by presenting two abstract machines which perform β reduction; one implements leftmost evaluation, the second implements applicative order evaluation.

The ideal situation would be to use a mixed strategy based on lazy evaluation (and thus avoiding the above problem) but using applicative order when it is safe to do so. We consider two analyses of λ-term programs; the common objective of both analyses is to provide information about the strictness of the terms. Such information can be used to optimise the evaluation of the terms because it allows us to detect when it is safe to use an innermost strategy.

In the final section we present an algorithm for inferring polymorphic types for terms.

8.1   Reduction machines

Both machines presented in this section execute a pure calculus; it would be possible to extend them to handle delta rules but the details are left for the reader to work out.

The principal problem that has to be addressed in implementing β reduction is the correct handling of substitution. A standard way of doing this is to maintain an environment (called an association list in the LISP meta-circular interpreter) which records the current values bound to free variables in an expression. We then have the problem of accessing the appropriate entry in the environment.

Rather than basing this section on the λ-calculus as presented earlier, we follow Curien in introducing a calculus of closures, $\lambda\rho$, which is an intermediate level between the λ-calculus and the abstract machines. The $\lambda\rho$-calculus is similar to the $\lambda\sigma$-calculus which is studied in more detail in Chapter 9; here we will just present enough details to make our presentation of the abstract machines comprehensible.

In contrast to the λ-calculus, substitution is an integral part of the $\lambda\rho$-calculus; we perform computations on closures which are objects consisting of a term and an environment. The terms use the de Bruijn notation (see Chapter 2) and consequently an occurrence of a free variable is an explicit index into the current environment (which is list structured); indexes start from 1. More formally, we use the following classes:

Definition 8.1 (Terms)
The class of Terms, $\mathcal{M}$, is the least class satisfying:

(1) $n \in \mathcal{M}$, *the de Bruijn indices.*
(2) *if $M, N \in \mathcal{M}$ then $(MN) \in \mathcal{M}$.*
(3) *if $M \in \mathcal{M}$ then $\lambda M \in \mathcal{M}$.*

Definition 8.2 (Closures)
The class of closures, $\mathcal{R}$, is the least class satisfying:

- *if $M \in \mathcal{M}$ and $u_1, \ldots, u_n \in \mathcal{R}$ (for n finite and $n \geq 0$) then we have $M[u_1; \ldots; u_n] \in \mathcal{R}$.*

In the last definition, the environment is the list of closures enclosed in $[\ldots]$. Notice that the definition includes the case of an empty environment ($n = 0$). In the following we will use $\cdot$ as the prefixing operation on environments. As stated earlier, our primary focus will be on computations on closures; these are specified by the following theory:

$$\textbf{Eval} \quad \frac{M[\rho] \overset{*}{\to} \lambda P[\nu]}{(MN)[\rho] \to P[N[\rho] \cdot \nu]}$$

$$\textbf{Access} \quad n[u_1; \ldots; u_m] \to u_n \quad (n \leq m)$$

$$\textbf{Env} \quad \frac{u_1 \overset{*}{\to} v_1 \ldots u_n \overset{*}{\to} v_n}{M[u_1; \ldots; u_n] \to M[v_1; \ldots; v_n]}$$

The first rule says that if the first term in an application reduces to an abstraction, then we can reduce the application to a closure consisting of the body of the abstraction and an environment which is the same as the abstraction environment with a new element prefixed to represent the argument closure. The third rule allows arbitrary reductions inside the environment component of a closure. Since there is no rule which tells how to reduce abstraction terms; this system will only reduce closures to weak head normal form.
An example of reduction according to these rules is:

$$\begin{aligned}
(\lambda.11)(\lambda.1)[] &\to 11[\lambda.1] \\
&\to 1[1[\lambda.1]] \quad \text{since } 1[\lambda.1] \to \lambda.1[] \\
&\to 1[\lambda.1] \quad \textbf{Access or Env} \\
&\to \lambda.1
\end{aligned}$$

It can be shown that this system is Church–Rosser; the interested reader is referred to the source material for details. As with our earlier presentation of $\to_\beta$, this system is neutral with respect to reduction strategy. We can impose a strategy by considering sub-systems which enforce an ordering on the sequence of reductions. We will now restrict $\lambda\rho$ in two different ways; the first motivates a lazy abstract machine (originally due to the French logician, Krivine) and the second leads to an eager machine which is similar to Curien's Categorical Abstract Machine (CAM).

8.1.1   Krivine's Machine

We consider a leftmost strategy for the calculus of closures. From consideration of the **Eval** rule it is clear that the environment is used to hold arguments. The arguments are never in the leftmost position, although they may become so after reduction, so we must prohibit the **Env** rule.

$$\textbf{LEval} \quad \frac{M[\rho] \xrightarrow{*}_l \lambda P[\nu]}{(MN)[\rho] \rightarrow_l P[N[\rho] \cdot \nu]}$$

$$\textbf{LAccess} \quad n[u_1; \ldots; u_m] \rightarrow_l u_n \quad (n \le m)$$

The system enforces a leftmost reduction strategy which, as with the earlier system, terminates with whnf. The strategy is implemented by an abstract machine which has two stacks and a code store. The first stack is used to represent the environment and the second is used as a temporary work space. A configuration of the machine is represented by a triple (ρ, M, S): an environment, term and stack. We use :: to represent an infix push operation on the stack. The machine is specified by the following four rules:

$$
\begin{array}{|ll|}
\hline
(\rho, MN, S) & \Rightarrow (\rho, M, N[\rho] :: S) \\
(\rho, \lambda M, u :: S) & \Rightarrow (u \cdot \rho, M, S) \\
(u \cdot \rho, n + 1, S) & \Rightarrow (\rho, n, S) \\
(M[\nu] \cdot \rho, 1, S) & \Rightarrow (\nu, M, S) \\
\hline
\end{array}
$$

The work space stack is used in the first rule to store the argument closure while the function of an application term is evaluated. The second rule constructs the term and environment specified by the conclusion of the **LEval** rule; notice that the argument is recovered from the work space stack where it was put by the first rule. The last two rules implement the **LAccess** rule by recursively searching down the environment.

Notice that the terminal states of this machine are either of the form $(\rho, \lambda M, [])$ or $([], n, S)$. States of the first form correspond to λ-terms of the form:

$$\lambda x.M$$

and states of the second form correspond to λ-terms of the form:

$$x M_1 \ldots M_n$$

where the tail terms are on the stack. These are precisely the two forms that a whnf can take.

An example of evaluation on this machine is the following transition sequence (to avoid overloading the reader with notation, we do not distinguish between a singleton list and its only element):

$$([], (\lambda.11)(\lambda.1), []) \Rightarrow ([], \lambda.11, \lambda.1) \Rightarrow$$
$$(\lambda.1, 11, []) \qquad \Rightarrow (\lambda.1, 1, 1[\lambda.1]) \Rightarrow$$
$$([], \lambda.1, 1[\lambda.1]) \qquad \Rightarrow (1[\lambda.1], 1, []) \quad \Rightarrow$$
$$(\lambda.1, 1, []) \qquad \Rightarrow ([], \lambda.1, [])$$

It is important to realise that this machine is lazy in the sense that values are evaluated on demand and then only as far as weak head normal form. In the functional programming literature the term "laziness" implies some form of sharing so that terms are evaluated at most once. The machine would be more complicated if we wanted to capture such sharing.

8.1.2   An Eager Machine

We can make the evaluation strategy more eager in a number of ways. The obvious way is to re-introduce the **Env** rule but this would allow the evaluation of arguments at arbitrary times. The solution that we adopt is to evaluate the arguments as part of the **Eval** rule. The eager strategy is defined by the following system:

$$\textbf{EEval} \quad \frac{M[\rho] \xrightarrow{*}_e \lambda P[\nu] \quad N[\rho] \xrightarrow{*}_e u}{(MN)[\rho] \rightarrow_e P[u \cdot \nu]}$$

$$\textbf{EAccess} \quad n[u_1; \ldots; u_m] \rightarrow_e u_n \quad (n \leq m)$$

The first rule now requires that the argument is evaluated, using the same environment as is used for evaluation of the function, before an application is reduced. As a result the environment will only contain values, not closures. This leads to some complication in the abstract machine because we now have to evaluate both the function and the argument before performing the application. We use the same configurations as the Krivine Machine but the Stack component now has markers, L and R, on it to record whether the code represents the left or right component of an application term. The abstract machine is specified by the following 6 rules:

(ρ, MN, S)	$\Rightarrow (\rho, M, L :: N[\rho] :: S)$
$(\rho, \lambda M, S)$	$\Rightarrow ([], , \lambda M[\rho] :: S)$
$(u \cdot \rho, n + 1, S)$	$\Rightarrow (\rho, n, S)$
$(u \cdot \rho, 1, S)$	$\Rightarrow ([], , u :: S)$
$([], , u :: L :: N[\rho] :: S)$	$\Rightarrow (\rho, N, R :: u :: S)$
$([], , u :: R :: \lambda M[\rho] :: S)$	$\Rightarrow (u \cdot \rho, M, S)$

The third and fourth rules concern environment access and are similar to the Krivine machine except no further evaluation is needed when the value is found. The first rule decomposes an application into its constituent parts. Both the second and the fourth rules leave a weak head normal form at the top of the work space stack. The last two rules concern configurations which have a null term and a value at the head of the work space stack; the marker below the top of stack indicates whether the top is a function value (L marker – rule 5) or an argument (R marker – rule 6). In the former case the new configuration initiates the evaluation of the argument. In the latter case, the body of the function below the R marker becomes the new term and the environment is appropriately updated.

Exercise 8.1.1 *What are the terminal configurations of this machine?*

An example of the evaluation of a term using this machine is the following:

$$
\begin{aligned}
([], (\lambda.11)(\lambda.1), []) &\Rightarrow ([], \lambda.11, L :: \lambda.1) &\Rightarrow \\
([], , \lambda.11 :: L :: \lambda.1) &\Rightarrow ([], \lambda.1, R :: \lambda.11) &\Rightarrow \\
([], , \lambda.1 :: R :: \lambda.11) &\Rightarrow (\lambda.1, 11, []) &\Rightarrow \\
(\lambda.1, 1, L :: 1[\lambda.1]) &\Rightarrow ([], , \lambda.1 :: L :: 1[\lambda.1]) &\Rightarrow \\
(\lambda.1, 1, R :: \lambda.1) &\Rightarrow ([], , \lambda.1 :: R :: \lambda.1) &\Rightarrow \\
(\lambda.1, 1, []) &\Rightarrow ([], , \lambda.1)
\end{aligned}
$$

Compare this to the earlier transition sequence.

Exercise 8.1.2
1. *Evaluate some examples using the two alternative mechanisms.*
2. *Investigate ways of adding δ-rules to the two machines; in particular consider the potential difficulties caused by adding conditional and fixed point operations to the eager machine.*

8.1.3   Correctness

We briefly consider the correctness of the abstract machines. We will concentrate on Krivine's machine; the correctness of the eager machine follows in an analogous way. Correctness follows from the following two lemmas.

Lemma 8.3

$$ M \xrightarrow{*}_l N \text{ implies } ([], M, []) \Rightarrow^* K $$

where N is a weak head normal form and K is a terminal machine state which corresponds to N.

Lemma 8.4

$$ ([], M, []) \Rightarrow^* K \text{ implies } M \xrightarrow{*}_l N $$

where K is a terminal configuration and N is a weak head normal form corresponding to K.

The proof of the first lemma involves an induction over the length of the derivation using the lazy evaluation proof system; the proof of the second lemma is by induction over the length of the computation sequence.

Exercise 8.1.3 *Prove these two lemmas.*

8.2   Needed Reductions

Consider the following term:

$$(\lambda xy.y)\underline{((\lambda x.xx)(\lambda x.xx))}_A \underline{((\lambda xy.x)z}_B w)$$

The subscripts identify two redexes. Redex A will be contracted in *some* reduction sequences to normal form. Redex B will be contracted in *all* reduction sequences to normal form. Based on these observations, we say that redex B is a *needed* redex. But can we detect such redexes? We start, as always, with some definitions:

Definition 8.5 *Let $R \in Sub(M)$ be a redex.*
R is needed *in M if every reduction sequence of M to nf reduces some residual of R.*
R is head-needed *in M if every reduction sequence of M to hnf reduces some residual of R.*

In fact, we will restrict our attention to determining the head-needed redexes in a term. These are of interest because this concept is closely related to the concept of strictness in functional languages.

Definition 8.6
A unary function is strict *in its argument if, whenever the argument is undefined (for example because of a non-terminating evaluation), then the result of the function is also undefined. This is often written:*

$$f(\bot) = \bot$$

There is an obvious generalisation to functions of more than one parameter.

The advantage that accrues from being able to identify which arguments a function is strict in is that those arguments can be evaluated using a more efficient strategy (any strategy will be normalising). The following result relates head-neededness and strictness:

Proposition 8.7 *For every context $C[]$ and redex R, the unary function associated with $C[]$ is strict iff R is head-needed in $C[R]$.*

Proof
We note that the unary function associated with $C[]$ is strict if $C[\Omega] = \Omega$ where Ω is a representative of the class of terms without hnf.
    Also note that $M \Leftrightarrow N$ is equivalent to $\neg M \Leftrightarrow \neg N$.

Now,

$$C[\Omega] \neq \Omega \Leftrightarrow C[\Omega] \text{ has a hnf}$$
$$\Leftrightarrow C[\Omega] \twoheadrightarrow_h \lambda x_1 \ldots x_n . x_i M_1 \ldots M_m$$
$$\Leftrightarrow C[R] \twoheadrightarrow_h \lambda x_1 \ldots x_n . x_i M_1^* \ldots M_m^*, \text{ without reducing R}$$
$$\Leftrightarrow R \text{ is not head-needed in } C[R]$$

$\square$

Unfortunately, it is undecidable whether a redex is (head-)needed or not; indeed, based on the equivalence of λ-definability and Turing computability established in Chapter 6, it can be shown that the problem is reducible to the Halting Problem for Turing Machines.

Before proceeding with the technical development, we pause for some examples of the above definitions:

In $\lambda xy.\mathbf{I}x(\mathbf{K}y(\mathbf{I}y))$:

- $\mathbf{I}x$ is head-needed and needed,
- $\mathbf{K}y$ is needed (but not head-needed),
- $(\lambda z.y)(\mathbf{I}y)$ is *created* (it is not a residual of any redex) by:

$$\mathbf{K}y(\mathbf{I}y) \rightarrow (\lambda z.y)(\mathbf{I}y)$$

it is needed in the created term.

We now present a non-computable "function" for finding head-needed redexes. The function is defined in terms of the following, which computes the *selection number* of a λ-term:

Definition 8.8 (Selection Numbers)

$$Sel(M) = \uparrow \ \textit{(undefined) if M has no hnf}$$
$$= 0 \ \textit{if M has a hnf with a free head variable}$$
$$= i \ (0 < i \leq n) \ \textit{if M has a hnf of the form:}$$
$$\lambda x_1 \ldots x_n . x_i M_1 \ldots M_m$$

This is not an algorithm since it is undecidable whether a term has a head normal form. $Sel(M)$ is a semi-decidable property; if it converges then we will know that M has an hnf of the indicated form. We use this function in the erasing function, $< \_ >: \Lambda \rightarrow \Lambda\bot$ (where $\Lambda\bot$ is the class of λ-terms constructed from the usual alphabet and the new distinguished symbol, $\bot$):

Definition 8.9

$$< x > \quad = x$$
$$< \lambda x.P > = \lambda x. < P >$$
$$< PQ > \quad = < P >< Q > \quad \textit{if } Sel(P) = 1$$
$$= < P > \bot \ \textit{otherwise}$$

The last clause is the important one. The intention is that subterms which are not needed get deleted; the argument subterm is only preserved if we know that the function subterm will reduce to an hnf that will force the argument into the head-redex position. Formalising this, we can make the following definitions:

Definition 8.10 *A redex is* visible *in* $< M >$ *if its leading* λ *appears in* $< M >$.

Definition 8.11 $R \in Sub(M)$ *is* <>-preserved *in* M *if* R *is visible in* $< M >$.

Example 8.12 *Let:*

$$M_1 \equiv \lambda w.(\lambda xy.yAB)((\lambda z.w)C)$$

$$M_2 \equiv \lambda w.(\lambda xy.xAB)((\lambda z.w)C)$$

Then:

$< M_1 > = \lambda w.(\lambda xy.y\bot\bot)\bot$
   since $Sel(y) = Sel(yA) = 0$ *and* $Sel(\lambda xy.yAB) = 2$
$< M_2 > = \lambda w.(\lambda xy.x\bot\bot)((\lambda z.w)\bot)$
   since $Sel(\lambda xy.xAB) = 1, Sel(x) = Sel(xA) = 0$ *and* $Sel(\lambda z.w) = 0$

Clearly, the redex $((\lambda z.w)C)$ *is visible in* $< M_2 >$ *but is not visible in* $< M_1 >$.

The main result concerning $< \_ >$ is the following:

Theorem 8.13 R *is* <>-*preserved in* $M \Rightarrow R$ *is head-needed in* M.

Proof
Induction on the structure of M.

$M \equiv x$, a variable: Then $R \equiv x$ and the result is trivial.

$M \equiv \lambda x.P$: $< M > = \lambda x. < P >$ and the result follows by the IH since $R \in Sub(P)$.

$M \equiv PQ$: There are three cases:

(1) $R \equiv PQ$: R is head-needed by definition.
(2) $R \in Sub(P)$:
   R is <>-preserved $\Rightarrow$ R is visible in $< P >$
                         $\Rightarrow$ R is head-needed in P, by IH
                         $\Rightarrow$ R is head-needed in M

(3) $R \in Sub(Q)$:

R is <>-preserved $\Rightarrow$ R is visible in $< Q >$ and $Sel(P) = 1$
$\qquad\qquad\qquad\quad\;\; \Rightarrow$ R is head-needed in Q and
$\qquad\qquad\qquad\qquad\quad P \twoheadrightarrow_h \lambda x_1 \ldots x_n.x_1 M_1 \ldots M_m$
$\qquad\qquad\qquad\quad\;\; \Rightarrow$ R is head-needed in M

$\square$

So far, so good; but *Sel* is not computable so we must devise a computable approximation. We define a function, $KSL : \Lambda\bot \to N^3 \cup \{(*, *, *)\}$. The interpretation of the results of this function is that if

$$KSL(M) = (k, s, j)$$

then M has a hnf of the form:

$$\lambda x_1 \ldots x_k.x_s M_1 \ldots M_j$$

and if

$$KSL(M) = (*, *, *)$$

then M may not have an hnf. Notice the uncertainty in the second case; this is the cost of the approximation — sometimes M will have an hnf but we will be unable to determine its form.

Definition 8.14 (The KSL Algorithm and $\oplus$)

$$
\begin{aligned}
KSL(\bot) \;\;\; &= (*, *, *)\\
KSL(x) \;\;\; &= (0, 0, 0)\\
KSL(\lambda x.P) &= KSL(P) + (1, 1, 0)\\
&\quad \text{if } x \in FV(< P >) \text{ or } FV(< P >) = \emptyset\\
&= KSL(P) + (1, 0, 0) \text{ otherwise}\\
KSL(PQ) \;\; &= KSL(P) \oplus KSL(Q)
\end{aligned}
$$

where we understand $+$ *to be defined on tuples component-wise with the following extension:*

$$x + * = * + x = *, x \text{ any number or } *$$

and $\oplus$ *is defined as follows:*

$$(*, *, *) \oplus (x, y, z) = (*, *, *) \tag{8.1}$$
$$(0, 0, j) \oplus (x, y, z) = (0, 0, j + 1) \tag{8.2}$$
$$(k + 1, 0, j) \oplus (x, y, z) = (k, 0, j) \tag{8.3}$$
$$(k + 1, 1, j) \oplus (*, *, *) = (*, *, *) \tag{8.4}$$
$$(k + 1, 1, j) \oplus (0, 0, j') = (k, 0, j + j') \tag{8.5}$$
$$(k + 1, n + 2, j) \oplus (x, y, z) = (k, n + 1, j) \tag{8.6}$$

$$(k+1,1,0) \oplus (k'+1,0,j') = (k+k'+1,0,j') \qquad (8.7)$$
$$(k+1,1,j+1) \oplus (k'+1,0,j') = (k+1,1,j) \oplus (k',0,j') \quad (8.8)$$
$$(k+1,1,0) \oplus (k'+1,1,j') = (k+k'+1,k+1,j') \qquad (8.9)$$
$$(k+1,1,j+1) \oplus (k'+1,1,j') = (*,*,*) \qquad (8.10)$$
$$(k+1,1,0) \oplus (k'+1,n'+2,j') = (k+k'+1,$$
$$k+n'+2,j') \qquad (8.11)$$
$$(k+1,1,j+1) \oplus (k'+1,n'+2,j') = (k+1,1,j) \oplus$$
$$(k',n'+1,j') \qquad (8.12)$$

(the clauses are numbered in the right-hand column for ease of reference).

Rather than give a formal proof of the correctness of these rules, for which we refer the reader to the source paper by Barendregt *et al*, we attempt to provide some motivation. Notice that KSL makes use of the $< \_ >$ function and since the new version of $< \_ >$ will use KSL, rather than Sel, they are mutually recursive. By inspection, the parameters involved in the mutual recursion are decreasing and consequently the recursion will "bottom out"; thus KSL and $< \_ >$ are total.

We start our consideration of KSL with the rule for abstraction. To understand this clause, we must know something about $FV(< P >)$. The only free variables appearing in $< P >$ must appear in subterms that will be head-needed in P, moreover there can only be one free variable and that will be the head variable of the hnf of P. Suppose that:

$$KSL(P) = (k,s,j)$$

then abstracting x will add one extra bound variable and will not add any extra terms in the "tail" of P. However, if $x \in FV(< P >)$ then following the above discussion, s must be 0 (since x is the head variable and it is free) and so by abstracting x we expect s to become 1. Alternatively, if $FV(< P >)$ is empty, then P is either $\perp$ (in which case it does not matter what we do!) or the head variable is bound in P, that is $1 \leq s \leq k$; in this case adding an extra bound variable should also require s to be increased by 1. In the case that $x \notin FV(< P >)$ and $FV(< P >)$ is not empty, then the head variable is still free and we should just increase k by 1, leaving s unchanged.

The operator $\oplus$ is a pseudo-application operator. The rules for $\oplus$ can be justified by consideration of the λ-terms which are represented by the KSL triples. We consider just three of the rules:

- (1) $(*,*,*) \oplus (x,y,z) = (*,*,*)$ is justified because $\perp M = \perp$ for any M.
- (2) $(0,0,j) \oplus (x,y,z) = (0,0,j+1)$ is justified because $(aM_1 \ldots M_j)M = aM_1 \ldots M_j M$

- (10) $(k+1, 1, j+1) \oplus (k'+1, 1, j') = (*, *, *)$:
  The right hand side represents the redex:

$$(\lambda x_1 \ldots x_{k+1}.x_1 M_1 \ldots M_{j+1})(\lambda y_1 \ldots y_{k'+1}.y_1 N_1 \ldots N_{j'})$$

which reduces in the following way:

$$\rightarrow \lambda x_2 \ldots x_{k+1}.(\lambda y_1 \ldots y_{k'+1}.y_1 N_1 \ldots N_{j'})M_1 \ldots M_{j+1}$$
$$\rightarrow \lambda x_2 \ldots x_{k+1} \ldots .M_1 \ldots$$

Whatever the respective values of k' and j are, the one thing that is certain about the last term above is that the term M_1 will appear in the head position. But we do not know anything about the term M_1 (the given triples tell us nothing about terms which appear in the tail of the associated terms); consequently, the only "safe" thing to do is to say that the composite term may not have a hnf (the term M_1 might be Ω for example). Rule (8.10) is the key rule which introduces the approximation discussed earlier.

Exercise 8.2.1
(a) Provide justifications for some of the other rules for $\oplus$.
(b) Rework the earlier examples which used Sel to use KSL.
(c) Identify a term M such that the second component of $KSL(M)$ is not equal to $Sel(M)$.

8.3   Strictness Analysis

The previous section detects (head-)needed reductions by consideration of reduction sequences; it is based on the proof theory of the λ-calculus. We can also use non-standard models to detect strictness.

   We recall from our discussion of needed reductions that a unary function is strict in its argument if:

$$f\perp = \perp$$

where we use the symbol $\perp$ to represent the undefined value. The above equation should be read "undefined arguments give undefined results". Unfortunately, as a consequence of the undecidability of the Halting Problem, we know that there is no algorithm to determine which arguments an arbitrary function is strict in. Instead, we have to settle for safe information; we will develop a technique which, like the KSL algorithm, will identify *some* of the arguments a function is strict in.

   The interpretations that we presented in Chapter 5 map terms to denotations which capture the complete information content of the term. Abstract Interpretation is a technique which involves mapping terms into some abstract model such that each term denotes an abstract value that just captures some property of the term (e.g. strictness). The abstract models are usually, although not always, finite; as a consequence abstract interpreters can be incorporated into optimising compilers to give a semantically sound basis for optimisations (in the case the model is infinite, appropriate approximation techniques have to be employed to ensure that the interpreter only has to access a finite portion of the model, otherwise the compiler would not terminate).

A simple example of an abstract interpretation is suggested by arithmetic. Suppose that we are posed the problem:

What is the sign of: $23 \times (-6) \times 15$?

The standard interpretation of integer arithmetic would map the strings of digits to integers, $-$ to negation and $\times$ to multiplication; it would determine that the above "term" denotes -2070 from which we can answer that the result is negative. Few readers will have taken this approach to answering the question; most will have used an abstract interpretation:

$$+ \otimes + = +$$
$$- \otimes - = +$$
$$- \otimes + = -$$
$$+ \otimes - = -$$

where each signed integer is mapped to its sign and we have interpreted multiplication by its *rule of signs* interpretation. We can thus answer that the sign of the result is negative since:

$$+ \otimes - \otimes + = -$$

As long as we only consider multiplication, we get exact answers; but even for this simple example we can see the need for safety, since if we add addition to the language, how can we answer questions of the form:

$$- \oplus + = ?$$

In the more general setting of abstract interpretation there seem to be three solutions.

First, we could restrict our attention to finite state systems or to properties which are decidable. In either case we are guaranteed to be able to develop an algorithm which always produces the right answer. At first sight, this solution may seem uninteresting – surely programs are usually infinitary and most properties are undecidable (strictness certainly is!)? Nevertheless, researchers working on *model checking* routinely restrict their attention to finite state systems (albeit with many millions of states!) and PASCAL type-checking is decidable but useful.

Second, we might seek "user" assistance when the analysis cannot proceed. This approach has been used successfully in program transformation systems. Unfortunately, the analysis is typically performed on some internal representation of the program; it may be difficult to seek assistance in terms of the source program and, as a result, the use of the analysis will be restricted to expert programmers.

Third, the analysis can be made fully automatic but we have to be prepared to accept that the information is inaccurate (but safe!).

We must establish some sort of correctness relationship between the abstract and standard models. The rule of signs example would give us incorrect information if we mapped every even number to + and every odd number to −. The relationship is usually defined by a pair of maps (α, γ), where α (called abstraction) maps from a (set of) standard value(s) to an abstract value and γ (called concretisation) maps from an abstract value to a set of standard values[1].

If we consider a property to be represented by the (standard denotations of) terms which satisfy the property, then correctness (safety) requires that:

$$\gamma(\llbracket Term \rrbracket^A) \subseteq Property \Rightarrow \llbracket Term \rrbracket^S \in Property$$

(where A is the abstract model and S is the standard one).

We will now turn our attention to strictness analysis. We will consider strictness analysis for a simple first-order functional language in which all parameters are integers or booleans:

$$
\begin{aligned}
prog &::= \textbf{let } def \textbf{ in } exp \\
def &::= f(variable_1, \ldots, variable_k) \Leftarrow exp \\
exp &::= f(exp_1, \ldots, exp_k) \mid \\
& \quad exp_1 \text{ binary-operation } exp_2 \mid \\
& \quad variable \mid \\
& \quad number \mid \\
& \quad \textbf{if } exp_1 \textbf{ then } exp_2 \textbf{ else } exp_3
\end{aligned}
$$

An example program, based on the ubiquitous factorial function, is:

$$\textbf{let } fac(n) \Leftarrow \textbf{if } n = 0 \textbf{ then } 1 \textbf{ else } n \times fac(n-1) \textbf{ in } fac(4)$$

A standard model for this language would look fairly similar to those of Chapter 5. The language is based on the λ-calculus; it is really just a syntactic sugaring of a λ-calculus with some constants. The standard interpretation will associate the standard denotation with integer constants and binary operations on them.

In strictness analysis, the booleans and integers denote elements of the two-point "domain":

$$\{0, 1\} \text{ with } 0 \sqsubseteq 1$$

where:

---

[1] An alternative approach is to use a (logical) relation to establish correctness. While this latter approach does lead to more perspicuous proofs, since our treatment will be informal, we will not treat either approach in detail.

- 0 represents the fact that the element is undefined
- 1 represents the fact that the element *may* be defined

There are *meet* ($\wedge$) and *join* ($\vee$) operations defined on this domain, in the following way:

$$0 \wedge 0 = 0$$
$$0 \wedge 1 = 0$$
$$1 \wedge 0 = 0$$
$$1 \wedge 1 = 1$$

$$0 \vee 0 = 0$$
$$0 \vee 1 = 1$$
$$1 \vee 0 = 1$$
$$1 \vee 1 = 1$$

Since the language is first-order, every expression denotes an object in the above domain. The strictness analysis abstract interpretation for expressions is as follows:

$$
\begin{aligned}
[\![f(exp_1, \ldots, exp_k)]\!]^{\#}\rho &= \rho(f)[\![exp_1]\!]^{\#}\rho \ldots [\![exp_k]\!]^{\#}\rho \\
[\![exp_1 \text{ binary-operation } exp_2]\!]^{\#}\rho &= [\![exp_1]\!]^{\#}\rho \wedge [\![exp_2]\!]^{\#}\rho \\
[\![variable]\!]^{\#}\rho &= \rho(variable) \\
[\![number]\!]^{\#}\rho &= 1 \\
[\![\text{if } exp_1 \text{ then } exp_2 \text{ else } exp_3]\!]^{\#}\rho &= \\
[\![exp_1]\!]^{\#}\rho \wedge ([\![exp_2]\!]^{\#}\rho \vee [\![exp_3]\!]^{\#}\rho)
\end{aligned}
$$

Some remarks about the above definition are in order:

(1) We assume that the environment is "initialised" with the denotation of the function, which is accomplished by the semantics of the definition discussed below.

(2) We assume all binary operations are strict in both arguments; consequently, we can map all such operations to the meet operation of our domain (which will evaluate to 0 — undefined — if either of the operands are 0).

(3) Any number is definitely defined so we map it to 1.

(4) The value of a conditional expression is definitely undefined if the predicate is (thus the meet operation again) but otherwise it may be as defined as the most-defined of the consequent or the alternative (hence the join).

Generally, we will be interested in analysing function definitions to determine whether the function is strict in any of its arguments. Since the function may be recursive we have to represent its semantics as the fixed point of some functional. The function will be represented by an abstraction term in the model. The appropriate semantics for definitions is:

$$[\![f(variable_1, \ldots, variable_k) \Leftarrow exp]\!]^{def}$$
$$=$$
$$\textbf{fix } \lambda\rho.\rho[f := (\lambda^* v_1 \ldots v_k.[\![exp]\!]^\# \rho[variable_i := v_i \mid 1 \leq i \leq k])]$$

where **fix** is a fixed point operator.

For the purposes of our presentation we can ignore the rather complex semantics of definitions and work with abstract recursion equations instead. Given a function definition:

$$f(variable_1, \ldots, variable_k) \Leftarrow exp$$

the abstract version of the function is just given by:

$$f^\#(variable_1, \ldots, variable_k) = exp^\#$$

$exp^\#$ is a syntactic term in which:

(1) Every function call has been replaced by a call of $f^\#$ with abstract versions of the argument expressions.

(2) Binary operators have been replaced by $\wedge$.

(3) Variables are left as they are.

(4) Constants are represented by 1.

(5) **if** e_1 **then** e_2 **else** e_3 is replaced by $e_1 \wedge (e_2 \vee e_3)$

The abstract version of the factorial function is:

$$fac^\#(n) = (n \wedge 1) \wedge (1 \vee (n \wedge fac^\#(n \wedge 1)))$$

The right hand side of the equation denotes an object in the two point domain. Using properties of join and meet, we can simplify the recursion equation to:

$$fac^\#(n) = n$$

The property of being undefined is expressed as the set:

$$\{\bot\}$$

The concretisation function for our strictness analysis is defined in the following way:

$$\gamma(0) = \{\bot\}$$
$$\gamma(1) = D,$$
$$\text{where } D \text{ is the carrier "set" of the standard model}$$

Consequently, the general correctness statement is translated to:

$$f^\# 1 \ldots 101 \ldots 1 = 0 \Rightarrow f v_1 \ldots v_{i-1} \bot v_{i+1} \ldots v_k = \bot$$
$$\text{for any values } v_j, 1 \leq j \leq k \text{ and } j \neq i$$

Since $fac^{\#}(0) = 0$, we can safely infer that fac is strict (assuming, which we will, that the strictness analysis is correct).

The factorial example is fortunate since the simplified form of the abstract recursion equation is non-recursive. We now consider an example where this is not the case:

let $dfac(m,n) \Leftarrow$ **if** $m = 0$ **then** n **else** $dfac(m-1, m \times n)$ **in** $dfac(4,1)$

The abstract recursion equation corresponding to $dfac$ is:

$$dfac^{\#}(m,n) = (m \wedge 1) \wedge (n \vee dfac^{\#}(m \wedge 1, m \wedge n))$$

after simplification the right-hand side becomes:

$$m \wedge (n \vee dfac^{\#}(m, m \wedge n))$$

and the equation is still recursive! In Chapter 6, we saw how the meaning of such an equation can be understood as the fixed point of an associated functional:

$$\lambda fmn.m \wedge (n \vee f(m, m \wedge n))$$

The fixed point in this particular case is a function of type $2 \times 2 \to 2$, where **2** is the two point domain, and so there is only a finite number of possibilities. An ad hoc way of finding the fixed point would be to try to solve the equation for $dfac^{\#}$ with each of the possibilities; a problem with this approach is that more than one of the possibilities may be a solution and then we will be faced with a choice[2]. A more methodical approach is an iterative approach which is inspired by the proof of Kleene's Fixed Point Theorem. We start with the assumption that dfac$^{\#}$ is everywhere undefined ($= \lambda mn.0$) and replace all calls to dfac$^{\#}$ in the right-hand side of the equation by this:

(Step 1)

$$dfac^{\#}(m,n) = m \wedge (n \vee ((\lambda mn.0)(m, m \wedge n))) = m \wedge n$$

On successive steps, we use the approximation to $dfac^{\#}$ generated by the previous step; when two successive steps generate the same approximation, the process terminates and the current approximation is the required fixed point:

---

[2]The best analysis would choose the least function, where the ordering on functions is induced from the ordering on **2**:

$$f \sqsubseteq g \Leftrightarrow \forall x, y. f(x,y) \sqsubseteq g(x,y)$$

(Step 2)

$$dfac^{\#}(m,n) = m \;\wedge\; (n \;\vee\; ((\lambda mn.m \;\wedge\; n)(m, m \;\wedge\; n)))$$
$$= m \;\wedge\; (n \;\vee\; (m \;\wedge\; n))$$
$$= m \;\wedge\; n$$

Consequently, the abstract version of *dfac* is:

$$dfac^{\#}(m,n) = m \;\wedge\; n$$

and *dfac* is strict in both arguments.

8.4 Polymorphic Type Inference

Many typed functional languages, although strongly typed, allow the definition of polymorphic functions. Recall from Chapter 7 that a polymorphic function is one which takes arguments of many different types but which behaves in the same way for each different type[3]. A simple example of a polymorphic function is:

$$map : (* \rightarrow **) \rightarrow [*] \rightarrow [**]$$

$$map\; f\; [] \quad = []$$
$$map\; f\; (a:x) = (f\;a) : (map\;f\;x)$$

The symbols $*$ and $**$ are used as type variables and [ ] is the list type constructor. One of the first programming languages to allow polymorphic functions was ML (see Chapter 7) and in this section we introduce an algorithm, due to Milner, which given an untyped function will either find a polymorphic type for it or indicate that it is untypable.

We will consider the following language *Exp* of expressions:

$$e ::= x \mid e\;e' \mid \lambda x.e \mid let\; x\; =\; e\; in\; e'$$

Types are constructed from type variables, typical representative α, primitive (ground) types, typical representative ι, and the function space constructor:

$$\tau ::= \alpha \mid \iota \mid \tau \rightarrow \tau$$

---

[3]The notion of polymorphism was introduced by Christopher Strachey. He distinguished two types of polymorphism; the type we have identified here is called *parametric polymorphism*, the other is called *ad hoc polymorphism*. In ad hoc polymorphism the function is allowed to do different things depending on the type of the argument; in modern terminology such a function is said to be *overloaded*. For example, a + operator which performs addition on integers and reals and concatenation on strings does very different things in each case and is thus overloaded. The $\lambda \cap$-calculus of Chapter 7 supports overloading. The polymorphic types presented here are less general than in the 2nd order polymorphic λ-calculus.

The algorithm will produce the principal type scheme for a term; type schemes have the following form:

$$\sigma ::= \tau \mid \forall \alpha . \sigma$$

We will use the shorthand $\forall \alpha_1 \ldots \alpha_n . \sigma$ for $\forall \alpha_1 \ldots \forall \alpha_n . \sigma$; the α_i are called *generic type variables*. A *monotype* is a type containing no type variables.

A substitution is a mapping from type variables to types. For a substitution S, we write:

$$S\sigma$$

to represent the type scheme obtained from σ by replacing each free occurrence of any variable in the domain of S by the corresponding element of the co-domain of S; the resultant type scheme is called an *instance* of σ. We sometimes write S explicitly as:

$$[\tau_1/\alpha_1, \ldots, \tau_n/\alpha_n]$$

meaning that τ_i $(1 \leq i \leq n)$ is substituted for α_i. Notice that the substitution operation may lead to variable capture if applied naively — we should adopt a variable convention.

In contrast to the notion of instance, a type scheme $\sigma = \forall \alpha_1 \ldots \alpha_m . \tau$ has a *generic instance* $\sigma' = \forall \beta_1 \ldots \beta_n . \tau'$ if $\tau' = [\tau_i/\alpha_i]\tau$ and the β_j are not free in σ; in this case we write $\sigma > \sigma'$. Notice that instantiation involves substitution for free variables while generic instantiation acts on bound variables.

We now present a formal system for type inference. The basic judgements, or assertions, in this system are of the form:

$$A \vdash e : \sigma$$

where A is a set of assumptions of the form:

$$x : \sigma' \text{ where } x \text{ is a variable}$$

The assertion should be read: "Under assumptions A, e has type σ". An assertion is closed if A and σ contain no free variables. The axioms and the rules are presented below:

Taut $A \vdash x : \sigma$ $(x : \sigma$ in $A)$

Inst $\dfrac{A \vdash e : \sigma}{A \vdash e : \sigma'}$ $(\sigma > \sigma')$

Gen $\dfrac{A \vdash e : \sigma}{A \vdash e : \forall \alpha.\sigma}$ $(\alpha$ not free in $A)$

Comb $\dfrac{A \vdash e : \tau' \to \tau \quad A \vdash e' : \tau'}{A \vdash (e\,e') : \tau}$

Abs $\dfrac{A_x \cup \{x : \tau'\} \vdash e : \tau}{A \vdash (\lambda x.e) : \tau' \to \tau}$

Let $\dfrac{A \vdash e : \sigma \quad A_x \cup \{x : \sigma\} \vdash e' : \tau}{A \vdash (let\ x = e\ in\ e') : \tau}$

The assumptions A_x used in **Abs** and **Let** denote the new assumptions derived from A by removing any assumption about x. The reader should compare these rules, particularly **Comb** and **Abs**, to the definition of λ^τ-terms in the last chapter. Notice that polymorphism is represented by type schemes; only the rules **Taut**, **Inst**, **Gen** and **Let** concern type schemes. Type inference amounts to a process of theorem proving in this formal system, for example:

$$\dfrac{\dfrac{x : \alpha \vdash x : \alpha \quad \textbf{Taut}}{\vdash (\lambda x.x) : \alpha \to \alpha \quad \textbf{Abs}}}{\vdash (\lambda x.x) : \forall \alpha.\alpha \to \alpha \quad \textbf{Gen}}$$

This (polymorphic) type associated with the identity function is the *most general type* for the identity function; all other possible types are generic instances of $\forall \alpha.\alpha \to \alpha$ – it is the largest type in the $>$-ordering.

We now present an algorithm for inferring types; the algorithm is Milner's $\mathcal{W}$ algorithm. The informal type of $\mathcal{W}$ is:

$$\text{Assumptions} \times \text{Exp} \to \text{Substitution} \times \text{Type}$$

and if:

$$\mathcal{W}(A, e) = (S, \tau)$$

then we have:

$$SA \vdash e : \tau$$

where substitutions are extended to assumption lists in the obvious way. In order to define $\mathcal{W}$, we will need two operations: unification and closure with respect to some assumptions.

Definition 8.15 *A* unifier *of two terms is a substitution which, when applied to the two terms, makes the terms equal. We will define an algorithm $\mathcal{U}$ which finds a unifier for two types τ and τ' or fails. Furthermore:*

(1) *If $\mathcal{U}(\tau, \tau') = V$ then $V\tau = V\tau'$
    i.e. V unifies τ and τ'*

(2) *If S unifies τ and τ' then $\mathcal{U}(\tau, \tau')$ returns some V and there is another substitution R such that*

$$S = RV$$

where composition of substitutions is done in the obvious way. This requirement amounts to stating that V does the least amount of work to equate the two terms; V is called the most general unifier.

(3) *V only involves variables in τ and τ'; no new variables are introduced during unification.*

The algorithm uses the notion of a *disagreement set*:

$$D(\tau, \tau') = \emptyset$$
$$\qquad \text{if } \tau = \tau'$$
$$= \{(\tau_1, \tau_1')\}$$
$$\qquad \text{if } \tau_1, \tau_1' \text{ are the "first" two subterms at which } \tau \text{ and } \tau' \text{ disagree}$$

In the second clause of the definition, we assume a depth-first traversal. Some examples may clarify this concept:

$$D(int \to int, int \to int) = \emptyset$$
$$D(\alpha \to \beta, \alpha \to \beta) = \emptyset$$
$$D(\alpha, \alpha \to \beta) = \{(\alpha, \alpha \to \beta)\}$$
$$D(\alpha \to \alpha, (int \to int) \to \beta) = \{(\alpha, int \to int)\}$$
$$D((int \to \alpha) \to \beta, (int \to int) \to \gamma) = \{(\alpha, int)\}$$

We now define $\mathcal{U}$ in terms of an auxiliary function which iterates with a substitution and the two types to find the unifier:

$$\mathcal{U}(\tau, \tau') \qquad = iterate(Id, \tau, \tau')$$

where

$iterate(V, \tau, \tau') =$ if $V\tau = V\tau'$
                      then V
                      elsif a is a variable that does not occur in b
                      then $iterate([b/a]V, \tau, \tau')$
                      elsif b is a variable that does not occur in a
                      then $iterate([a/b]V, \tau, \tau')$
                      else FAIL
                      where $\{(a, b)\} = D(V\tau, V\tau')$

The reader should, at least informally, verify that this definition does meet the earlier specification.

Exercise 8.4.1 *Show that*

$$\mathcal{U}(\beta \rightarrow \gamma, \gamma \rightarrow \epsilon) = [\epsilon/\gamma, \gamma/\beta]$$

The closure of a type results in a type where some free variables are quantified; more formally:

Definition 8.16 *The* closure *of a type τ with respect to some assumptions A involves making any free variables of τ which are not free in A into generic type variables. We write the closure as $\overline{A}(\tau)$. Thus:*

$$\overline{A}(\tau) = \forall \alpha_1 \ldots \alpha_n.\tau$$

where $\alpha_1, \ldots, \alpha_n$ are the type variables occurring free in τ but not in A.

We now define $\mathcal{W}$:

$\mathcal{W}(A, e) = (S, \tau)$ where

(i) If $e \equiv x$ and $x : \forall \alpha_1 \ldots \alpha_n.\tau' \in A$ then $S = Id$ and $\tau = [\beta_i/\alpha_i]\tau'$ with the β_i new.

(ii) If $e \equiv e_1 e_2$:
let $\mathcal{W}(A, e_1) = (S_1, \tau_1)$ and
$\mathcal{W}(S_1 A, e_2) = (S_2, \tau_2)$
and $\mathcal{U}(S_2 \tau_1, \tau_2 \rightarrow \beta) = V$ where β is new
then $S = V S_2 S_1$ and $\tau = V\beta$.

(iii) If $e \equiv \lambda x.e_1$:
let β be a new type variable and $\mathcal{W}(A_x \cup \{x : \beta\}, e_1) = (S_1, \tau_1)$
then $S = S_1$ and $\tau = S_1\beta \rightarrow \tau_1$.

(iv) If $e \equiv let\ x = e_1\ in\ e_2$:
let $\mathcal{W}(A, e_1) = (S_1, \tau_1)$ and

$$\mathcal{W}(S_1 A_x \cup \{x : \overline{S_1 A}(\tau_1)\}, e_2) = (S_2, \tau_2)$$
then $S = S_2 S_1$ and $\tau = \tau_2$.

(v) Otherwise $\mathcal{W}$ fails.

We now state and prove several important properties of this algorithm.

Proposition 8.17 *If S is a substitution and $A \vdash e : \sigma$ holds then $SA \vdash e : S\sigma$ also holds. Moreover if there is a derivation of $A \vdash e : \sigma$ of height n then there is also a derivation of $SA \vdash e : S\sigma$ of height less than or equal to n.*

Proof by induction on the height n of the derivation of $A \vdash e : \sigma$.

Basis: the only derivations of height zero are instances of **Taut**, i.e. $A \vdash e : \sigma$ with $x : \sigma$ in A. Then $x : S\sigma$ is in SA and we also have $SA \vdash e : S\sigma$.

Induction step: the most difficult case is when the last step of the derivation involves the use the **Gen** rule. In this case σ is of the form $\forall \alpha.\sigma'$. The antecedent is $A \vdash e : \sigma'$ and α is not free in A. By the inductive hypothesis $SA \vdash e : S\sigma'$ but we can no longer use the **Gen** rule because α may be free in SA. Instead we introduce a new type variable α'. Now by the induction hypothesis:

$$S[\alpha'/\alpha]A \vdash e : S[\alpha'/\alpha]\sigma'$$

and since neither α or α' occur in A:

$$SA \vdash e : S[\alpha'/\alpha]\sigma'$$

and now the **Gen** rule applies and we have the result (modulo renaming of generic variables).

$\square$

Exercise 8.4.2
1. Prove that for any type schemes σ and σ' and any substitution S, if $\sigma > \sigma'$ then $S\sigma > S\sigma'$.
2. Complete the proof of the previous proposition.

Theorem 8.18 (Soundness of $\mathcal{W}$)
If

$$\mathcal{W}(A, e) = (S, \tau)$$

then

$$SA \vdash e : \tau$$

which is just the property that we required in the specification of $\mathcal{W}$.

Proof by induction on e.

We just consider the application e e'. By the induction hypothesis we have:

$$S_1 A \vdash e : \tau_1$$

and

$$S_2 S_1 A \vdash e' : \tau_2$$

From the proposition we have:

$$V S_2 S_1 A \vdash e : V S_2 \tau_1$$

and

$$V S_2 S_1 A \vdash e' : V \tau_2$$

Now $V S_2 \tau_1$ is equal to $V \tau_2 \rightarrow V \beta$ by the unification algorithm. Thus we can combine the previous two judgements with the **Comb** rule to give:

$$V S_2 S_1 A \vdash e\ e' : V \beta$$

as required.   □

Exercise 8.4.3 *Complete the above proof.*

Given A and e, σ_p is a *principal type scheme* of e under A if and only if:

- $A \vdash e : \sigma_p$
- Any other σ for which $A \vdash e : \sigma$ is a generic instance of σ_p.

Soundness states (approximately) that any types inferred by $\mathcal{W}$ can be inferred using the inference system. An equally important property is *completeness*, which means that any type that can be inferred by the inference system can be found by $\mathcal{W}$ (again approximately). We state two versions of completeness without proof; see the seminal paper by Damas and Milner for details.

1. **Completeness of $\mathcal{W}$:** Given A and e, let A' be an instance of A and σ a type scheme such that $A' \vdash e : \sigma$ then:

   - $\mathcal{W}(A, e)$ succeeds
   - If $\mathcal{W}(A, e) = (S, \tau)$ then for some substitution R:

   $$A' = RSA$$

   and $\overline{RSA}(\tau) > \sigma$

2. **Completeness (no free type variables) of $\mathcal{W}$:** If $A \vdash e : \sigma$, for some σ, then $\mathcal{W}$ computes a principal type scheme for e under A.

Property 2 is actually a simple corollary of Property 1.
We give an example of the application of $\mathcal{W}$:

Example 8.19 $\mathcal{W}(\{\}, \lambda f x . f(f x))$

by (iii) we need to evaluate $\mathcal{W}(\{f : \alpha\}, \lambda x.f(fx))$ *where* α *is a new type variable.*

Thus by (iii) again, we need to evaluate $\mathcal{W}(\{x : \beta, f : \alpha\}, f(fx))$ *where* β *is a new variable.*

To evaluate $\mathcal{W}(\{x : \beta, f : \alpha\}, f(fx))$, *by (ii) we should evaluate* $\mathcal{W}(\{x : \beta, f : \alpha\}, f)$ *which is:*

$$(Id, \alpha) \text{ by (i)} \qquad\qquad (*)$$

Then we evaluate $\mathcal{W}(Id\{x : \beta, f : \alpha\}, fx)$:

$$
\begin{aligned}
\mathcal{W}(Id\{x : \beta, f : \alpha\}, f) &= (Id, \alpha) \text{ by (i)} \\
\mathcal{W}(IdId\{x : \beta, f : \alpha\}, x) &= (Id, \beta) \text{ by (i)} \\
\mathcal{U}(\alpha, \beta \to \gamma) &= [\beta \to \gamma/\alpha] \text{ where } \gamma \text{ is new}
\end{aligned}
$$

thus:

$$\mathcal{W}(Id\{x : \beta, f : \alpha\}, fx) = ([\beta \to \gamma/\alpha], \gamma) \qquad\qquad (**)$$

Next have to unify (*) and (**) as specified in (ii):

$$
\begin{aligned}
\mathcal{U}([\beta \to \gamma/\alpha]\alpha, \gamma \to \epsilon) &= \mathcal{U}(\beta \to \gamma, \gamma \to \epsilon) \text{ where } \epsilon \text{ is new} \\
&= [\epsilon/\gamma, \gamma/\beta]
\end{aligned}
$$

Thus:

$$
\begin{aligned}
\mathcal{W}(\{x : \beta, f : \alpha\}, f(fx)) &= ([\epsilon/\gamma, \gamma/\beta, \beta \to \gamma/\alpha], \epsilon) \text{ by (ii)} \\
\mathcal{W}(\{f : \alpha\}, \lambda x.f(fx)) &= ([\epsilon/\gamma, \gamma/\beta, \beta \to \gamma/\alpha], \epsilon \to \epsilon) \text{ by (ii)}
\end{aligned}
$$

and finally:

$$\mathcal{W}(\{\}, \lambda fx.f(fx)) = ([\epsilon/\gamma, \gamma/\beta, \beta \to \gamma/\alpha], (\epsilon \to \epsilon) \to \epsilon \to \epsilon)$$

by (ii) as expected!

Exercise 8.4.4 *Use* $\mathcal{W}$ *to infer the type of* $\lambda xyz.xz(yz)$.

We conclude this section by noting the importance of the let-construct in the language. In a type-free setting:

$$let \ x = e \ in \ e'$$

is just syntactic sugar for:

$$(\lambda x.e')e$$

This is no longer true when we use $\mathcal{W}$ to infer types. The let-construct introduces polymorphic functions; thus:

$$let \ f = \lambda x.x \ in \dots f \ true \dots f \ 1 \dots$$

can be validly typed because f will be given type $\forall \alpha.\alpha \to \alpha$ (because of the closure operator in (iv)) which can then be instantiated to both *bool* → *bool* and *int* → *int*. However:

$$(\lambda f. \dots f \ true \dots f \ 1 \dots)(\lambda x.x)$$

cannot be validly typed because $\lambda x.x$ is given type $\alpha \to \alpha$ and α can only be instantiated to one type.

8.5   Summary

In this chapter we have studied more practical aspects of the λ-calculi. The topics we have presented should have given the reader some idea of how the theory of the preceding chapters is put to use in the implementation of (functional) programming languages. The abstract machines are closely related to the implementation techniques that are used in practical functional programming systems. The development of efficient methods of program analysis is state-of-the-art research in advanced compiling technology. Most of the modern functional languages allow the definition of polymorphic functions and use type checking algorithms based on the one presented in the last section.

9

Other Calculi

Overview

In this chapter we present three other calculi which have been proposed in the last few years. Each addresses a different deficiency of the pure calculus that has been our main object of study. This chapter is slightly different in style compared to the earlier chapters; we cover a lot of material with few examples or exercises. We have chosen to emphasise the proof theory of the calculi — the interested reader is urged to consult the original source material for details of models and more motivational examples.

The three calculi are:

Abramsky's Lazy λ-calculus: The standard theory fails to distinguish between terms which have markedly different behaviours in any lazy implementation of the calculus. The lazy λ-calculus gives a more faithful account of such implementations.

Boudol's γ-calculus: The classical λ-calculus is essentially a calculus for describing "sequential" programs. The γ-calculus is a process-based calculus which extends the λ-calculus with non-deterministic operators. The result is that we can construct γ-terms which denote computations which are not representable in the λ-calculus.

The $\lambda\sigma$-calculus: The $\lambda\sigma$-calculus has been proposed by Abadi, Cardelli, Curien and Lévy. In contrast to the classical λ-calculus where substitution is extra-logical (recall Chapter 2), in the $\lambda\sigma$-calculus substitutions are dealt with as an explicit part of the calculus. Since the main problem in any implementation of the λ-calculus is the correct handling of substitution, this new calculus gives important insights into abstract machine structures (amongst other things).

9.1   The Lazy λ-calculus

The standard models of the λ-calculus equate terms which do not have a head normal form (refer to the discussion in Chapter 3). As a consequence, for any such model $\mathcal{M}$ we have:

$$\mathcal{M} \models \Omega = \lambda x.\Omega$$

Lazy evaluation, however, distinguishes between these two terms; Ω leads to an infinite reduction sequence whereas $\lambda x.\Omega$ is a well-defined value. This difference results from the fact that the lazy evaluation of a term stops at *weak head normal form*:

Definition 9.1 *A term is a weak head normal form (whnf) if:*
either *(i) it is of the form* $\lambda x.M$
or *(ii) it is of the form* $x M_1 \ldots M_m$ *for* $m \geq 0$

Notice that Ω has no whnf, whereas $\lambda x.\Omega$ is a whnf. In the lazy λ-calculus, we equate terms which have the same whnf and equate all terms which do not have a whnf (this last class of terms being used to represent the "undefined" computations).

Abramsky develops a theory, $\lambda \ell$, and models of the lazy λ-calculus. We will concentrate on the theory; the interested reader is referred to Abramsky's papers for details of the models.

9.1.1   The theory of the lazy λ-calculus

The terms of the lazy λ-calculus are the same as the terms of the untyped λ-calculus, Λ.

The theory is defined via an auxiliary notion of convergence:

Definition 9.2 (Convergence)
For $M, N \in \Lambda^0$, *M converges to* principal whnf *N, written $M \Downarrow N$, if $M \Downarrow N$ is a theorem of the following theory:*

$$\lambda x.M \Downarrow \lambda x.M$$

$$\frac{M \Downarrow \lambda x.P \quad P[x := N] \Downarrow Q}{MN \Downarrow Q}$$

We will write $M \Downarrow$ and say that M converges if:

$$\exists N. M \Downarrow N$$

and we will write $M \Uparrow$ (M diverges) if $\neg(M \Downarrow)$.

Notice that the previous definition is for closed terms only. The whnf of a closed term is also closed and must therefore be an abstraction term. Such a whnf does not tell us very much about the behaviour of the term; the body of the abstraction may involve an arbitrary number of redexes which is in contrast to the classical situation where we deal with normal forms. We may gain information about a term by performing a sequence of *experiments* on the term[1] — we can "unravel" the whnf step by step by providing successive arguments and evaluating to whnf. The reader should compare this process to the construction of the Böhm-like tree of a term presented in Chapter 5.

---

[1] Readers familiar with Milner's CCS and related process algebras will find the following very familiar.

We establish a sequence of relations, $\{\preceq_k\}_{k \in \omega}$ on Λ^0:

$$M \preceq_0 N$$

$$M \preceq_{k+1} N \equiv$$
$$M \Downarrow \lambda x.M_1 \Rightarrow \exists N_1.[N \Downarrow \lambda y.N_1 \ \& \ \forall P \in \Lambda^0.[M_1[x := P] \preceq_k N_1[y := P]]]$$

So we always have $M \preceq_0 N$; if we don't perform any experiments, we cannot differentiate between any terms.

We now define the following relationship between terms:

Definition 9.3

$$M \preceq^B N \equiv \forall k \in \omega.M \preceq_k N$$

The relation $\preceq^B$ is an applicative bisimulation[2].

$\preceq^B$ is extended to all terms, Λ in the standard way:

$$M \preceq^B N \equiv \forall \sigma : Var \to \Lambda^0.M\sigma \preceq^B N\sigma$$

where σ is a substitution (of closed terms for variables) and $X\sigma$ represents a closed term in which all free variables in X have been replaced by closed terms as specified by σ (compare with the notation introduced in Chapter 7). $\preceq^B$ satisfies the following:

$$M \preceq^B N \Leftrightarrow$$

$$M \Downarrow \lambda x.P \Rightarrow \exists Q.[N \Downarrow \lambda x.Q \ \& \ \forall L \in \Lambda^0.[P[x := L] \preceq^B Q[x := L]]]$$

We write $M \sim^B N$ if $M \preceq^B N$ and $N \preceq^B M$.

Given our informal description of the $\preceq_k$ relations and the above we have the following result:

Proposition 9.4

$$M \preceq^B N \Leftrightarrow \forall \vec{P} \subseteq \Lambda^0.M\vec{P} \Downarrow \Rightarrow N\vec{P} \Downarrow$$

An alternative characterisation of applicative bisimulation is given by the following contextual congruence:

Definition 9.5 *For $M, N \in \Lambda^0$:*

$$M \preceq^C N \equiv \forall C[] \in \Lambda^0.C[M] \Downarrow \Rightarrow C[N] \Downarrow$$

$\preceq^C$ can be extended to all terms in the same way as $\preceq^B$. The equivalence of the two notions is proved in the following proposition (the proof of which follows the approach of Ong and Abramsky):

Proposition 9.6 $\preceq^B = \preceq^C$

---

[2]Compare the definition of $\preceq^B$ to that of bisimulation used in CCS — the notion of applicative bisimulation is really a *simulation* relation in that setting. This has been acknowledged by Ong and Abramsky in their later writings. See also the next section.

Proof

We need to show the following:

$$M \preceq^B N \Leftrightarrow M \preceq^C N$$

($\Leftarrow$)

Use the definition of $\preceq^C$ and Proposition 9.4 with contexts $[]\vec{P}$.

($\Rightarrow$)

Given $M, N \in \Lambda^0$, we show that:

$$M \preceq^B N \Rightarrow \forall C[] \in \Lambda^0 . C[M] \Downarrow \Rightarrow C[N] \Downarrow$$

by induction on the number of steps that it takes for $C[M]$ to converge. The base case is obvious. For the inductive case, we need only consider the following contexts:

(1) $C[] \equiv (\lambda x.P[])(Q[])\vec{R}[]$,

(2) $C[] \equiv [](P[])\vec{Q}[]$

These are sufficient to allow us to focus on the first step of leftmost reduction.

Here, we just consider the first case. Suppose $C[M]$ converges in $l+1$ steps. Define:

$$D[] \equiv (P[])[x := Q[]]\vec{R}[]$$

Then it is easy to see that:

$$C[M] \to_{lm} D[M]$$

where $\to_{lm}$ is one-step leftmost reduction and we now have that $D[M]$ converges in l steps. Thus by the induction hypothesis we have that $D[N] \Downarrow$ which implies $C[N] \Downarrow$. $\square$

Exercise 9.1.1 *Complete the above proof, i.e. the second case in the induction. You should start with* $M \equiv (\lambda x.U)\vec{V}$.

From now on we will write $\preceq$ instead of $\preceq^B$. The following establishes some basic properties of $\preceq$:

Proposition 9.7 *For all* $M, N, P \in \Lambda$:

(1) $M \preceq M$

(2) $M \preceq N \& N \preceq P \Rightarrow M \preceq P$

(3) $M \preceq N \Rightarrow M[x := P] \preceq N[x := P]$

(4) $M \preceq N \Rightarrow P[x := M] \preceq P[x := N]$

(5) $\lambda x.M \sim \lambda y.M[x := y] \quad y \notin (FV M)$

(6) $M \preceq N \Rightarrow \lambda x.M \preceq \lambda x.N$

(7) $M_i \preceq N_i (i = 1, 2) \Rightarrow M_1 M_2 \preceq N_1 N_2$

Proof

We just prove (4), which is equivalent to:

$$M \preceq^C N \Rightarrow P[x := M] \preceq^C P[x := N]$$

Bound variables in P are renamed to avoid clashes with M and N. P is transformed to a context $P[]$ by replacing instances of the (bound) variable x by $[]$; thus

$$P[x := M] = P[M] \text{ and } P[x := N] = P[N]$$

Let $C[] \in \Lambda^0$ and $\sigma \in Var \to \Lambda^0$ be given. Let $C_1[] \equiv C[P[]\sigma]$. $M \preceq^C N$ implies:

$$C_1[M\sigma] \Downarrow \Rightarrow C_1[N\sigma] \Downarrow$$

which, since $(P[x := M])\sigma = (P[]\sigma)[M\sigma]$, gives the required result. $\square$

Exercise 9.1.2 *Complete the above proof.*

The theory of the lazy λ-calculus, $\lambda\ell$, has two types of formulae:

$$M \sqsubseteq N \text{ and } M = N$$

where:

$$\lambda\ell \vdash M \sqsubseteq N \equiv M \preceq^B N$$
$$\lambda\ell \vdash M = N \equiv M \sim^B N$$

We close this subsection with a proposition which establishes some basic properties of the theory $\lambda\ell$:

Proposition 9.8

(1) λ is included in $\lambda\ell$, in particular:

$$\lambda\ell \vdash (\lambda x.M)N = M[x := N]$$

i.e. the rule (β) is satisfied.

(2) Ω is the least element for $\sqsubseteq$

(3) (η) is not valid in $\lambda\ell$, e.g.:

$$\lambda\ell \nvdash \lambda x.\Omega x = \Omega$$

but we do have the following conditional version of η:

$$(\Downarrow \eta) \quad \lambda\ell \vdash \lambda x.Mx = M \quad (M \Downarrow, x \notin FV(M))$$

where $M \Downarrow \equiv \forall \sigma \in Var \to \Lambda^0.(M\sigma) \Downarrow$.

(4) **YK** is the greatest element for $\sqsubseteq$.

Exercise 9.1.3 *Prove this proposition.*

9.2   The γ-calculus

We now consider an extension of the λ-calculus for concurrent and communicating systems, Boudol's γ-calculus. In the γ-calculus terms denote processes which are able to communicate via named ports. In common with the previous section, the relationship between terms is established by a notion of bisimulation. We start by presenting the syntax and basic theory of the γ-calculus and close the section by considering the relationship to the λ-calculus.

9.2.1   The theory of the γ-calculus

Since communication between terms is via named ports, it is reasonable to consider the ports to be *binders* which play a similar rôle to λ in the λ-calculus. The class of binders, $\mathcal{B}$, is defined over the alphabet:

$x, y, \ldots$	variables
$\alpha, \beta, \ldots$	port names
$(,)$	parentheses
ε	empty binder
$\mid$	interleave
.	sequence

Definition 9.9 *The class of binders $\mathcal{B}$ is the least class such that:*

(1) $\varepsilon \in \mathcal{B}$

(2) $\alpha x \in \mathcal{B}$ *where α is any port name and x is any variable.*

(3) *If $\rho_1, \rho_2 \in \mathcal{B}$ then $(\rho_1.\rho_2)$, $(\rho_1 \mid \rho_2) \in \mathcal{B}$*

The major innovation is the ability to interleave binders; the intention of this construction is that the bindings can occur in any order. One significant use of this is when the binders have the same port names which enables the encoding of a non-deterministic choice:

$$< \lambda x \mid \lambda y > .x$$

(Although we have not discussed the syntax of terms, it should be clear what is intended here: this defines a process which accepts two inputs on the λ port which are non-deterministically bound to x and y; the value bound to x is returned.)

Certain binders have the same effect; in particular it is reasonable to expect ε to be an identity for both sequencing and interleaving:

$$(\rho.\varepsilon) \; = \rho = (\varepsilon.\rho)$$
$$(\rho \mid \varepsilon) = \rho = (\varepsilon \mid \rho)$$

We take $\doteq$ to be the congruence generated by these equations and this establishes the syntactic equality over binders. We will use this technique again later, so we pause to revise precisely what is meant by the last sentence. First, it is possible to define the notion of a binder context, $B[]$ – a binder with holes; the definition of this is straightforward from the definition of $\mathcal{B}$. The congruence is then generated from the above equations and the following rule:

$$\rho \doteq \rho' \Rightarrow B[\rho] \doteq B[\rho']$$

The purpose of binders is to bind a set of variables; by analogy with the λ-calculus, we can define a function BV which, when applied to a binder, produces the set of variables bound by the binder:

Definition 9.10 *The set of bound variables introduced by a binder is defined inductively via the function* $BV : \mathcal{B} \to \wp(Var)$:

$$\begin{aligned}
BV(\varepsilon) &= \varnothing \\
BV(\alpha x) &= \{x\} \\
BV(\rho_1.\rho_2) &= BV(\rho_1) \cup BV(\rho_2) \\
BV(\rho_1 \mid \rho_2) &= BV(\rho_1) \cup BV(\rho_2)
\end{aligned}$$

We now turn to the syntax of terms. Terms are constructed from binders and expressions, and consequently the alphabet used is the same as for binders plus:

$\mathbb{1}$	idle
$\bar{\alpha}, \bar{\beta}$	complemented port names
$<, >$	
$\odot$	cooperation

Definition 9.11 *The class of γ-terms,* Γ, *is the least class such that:*

(1) $x \in \Gamma$, *where* x *is any variable*
(2) $\mathbb{1} \in \Gamma$
(3) *If* $p, p_1, p_2 \in \Gamma$ *and* $\rho \in \mathcal{B}$:
    (a) $\bar{\alpha} p \in \Gamma$
    (b) $< \rho > .p \in \Gamma$
    (c) $(p_1 \odot p_2) \in \Gamma$
    (d) $(p_1 \mid p_2) \in \Gamma$

Before we continue with our formal presentation of the γ-calculus, some remarks concerning the intuitive meanings of terms may be in order. $\mathbb{1}$ is used to denote the idle process which is incapable of any further interaction. Terms of the form $\bar{\alpha} p$ are able to transmit the value of p to a port with name α. $(p \mid q)$ represents the arbitrary interleaving of the "evaluation" of p and q (with no interaction possible). Finally, $(p \odot q)$ denotes the cooperation of p and q, which enables p and q to communicate across common ports.

The definition of free variables is straightforward:

$$\begin{aligned}
FV(\mathbb{1}) &= \emptyset \\
FV(x) &= \{x\} \\
FV(\bar{a}p) &= FV(p) \\
FV(<\rho>.p) &= FV(p) - BV(\rho) \\
FV(p \odot q) &= FV(p) \cup FV(q) \\
FV(p \mid q) &= FV(p) \cup FV(q)
\end{aligned}$$

As with the bindings, we consider the class of terms modulo syntactic equality, $\equiv$, which is the congruence generated by:

$$(p \odot \mathbb{1}) = p = (\mathbb{1} \odot p)$$
$$(p \mid \mathbb{1}) = p = (\mathbb{1} \mid p)$$
$$<\varepsilon>.p = p$$
$$<\rho>.p = <\rho\prime>.p \text{ if } \rho \doteq \rho\prime$$
$$<\rho>.p = <\rho[x := y]>.p[x := y] \text{ if } x \in BV(\rho) \text{ and } y \notin FV(p) \cup BV(\rho)$$

Notice that the last equation corresponds to α-congruence in the λ-calculus.

Proposition 9.12 $\equiv$ *is substitutive, that is:*

$$p \equiv q \Rightarrow p\sigma \equiv q\sigma$$

for any substitution σ.

Proof
(by induction on the definition of $\equiv$).   □

Exercise 9.2.1 *Complete the proof of the above proposition.*

Definition 9.13 p *is* terminated *or* idle, *written* $p\dagger$, *if* $p \equiv \mathbb{1}$.

We are now ready to define a relationship between terms which is similar to reduction in λ-calculus. We need to take a certain amount of care in defining this relationship; in the setting of the γ-calculus it is reasonable that any term of the form:

$$\bar{a}p$$

should be able to pass the value of p to α and then become idle ($\equiv \mathbb{1}$). If we define "reduction" as a binary relation on terms, there is no way of distinguishing any of the output terms: they all reduce to $\mathbb{1}$ in one step and are thus "convertible". To distinguish such terms, we have to observe the communications as well as the end result. This leads to the idea of a labelled transition (reduction) relation between terms; a notion that is commonly used in the semantics of concurrent languages.

We will define a transition relation $\xrightarrow{a}: \Gamma \times \mathcal{A} \times \Gamma$ and write $p \xrightarrow{a} p'$ if p reduces to p' in one step via the *action a*. We consider three types of action:

$$\alpha_p \qquad \text{receive } p \text{ on port } \alpha$$
$$\bar{\alpha}_p \qquad \text{send } p \text{ to port } \alpha$$
$$\tau \qquad \text{silent action}$$

Formally, the class of actions, $\mathcal{A}$, is

$$(N \times \Gamma) \cup (\Gamma \times N) \cup \{\tau\}$$

where N is the set of port names and the first component corresponds to receiving and the second corresponds to sending actions. The τ-action represents an action which is not directly observable because it arises as the result of (private) cooperation between two terms; readers familiar with Milner's CCS or other process algebras will realise that τ-actions play the same rôle there.

Definition 9.14 *Two actions a and b are* complementary, *written* $a \frown b$, *if* $a = \alpha_p$ *and* $b = \bar{\alpha}_p$ *or vice versa.*

Finally, before presenting the relation on terms, we introduce an auxiliary labelled transition system for bindings. In this transition system, labels are of the form: $\alpha_{x,p}$, meaning that x is bound to p as a result of a communication on port α. The transition relation is the least one satisfying:

$$\alpha x \xrightarrow{\alpha_{x,p}} \varepsilon \qquad p \in \Gamma$$

$$\frac{\rho \xrightarrow{a} \rho'}{(\rho.\rho'') \xrightarrow{a} (\rho'.\rho'')}$$

$$\frac{\rho \dot{=} \varepsilon \quad \rho' \xrightarrow{a} \rho''}{(\rho.\rho') \xrightarrow{a} \rho''}$$

$$\frac{\rho \xrightarrow{a} \rho'}{(\rho \mid \rho'') \xrightarrow{a} (\rho' \mid \rho'')}$$

$$\frac{\rho \xrightarrow{a} \rho'}{(\rho'' \mid \rho) \xrightarrow{a} (\rho'' \mid \rho')}$$

The transition relation on terms is defined as the least subset of $\Gamma \times \mathcal{A} \times \Gamma$ defined by:

$$\bar{\alpha}p \xrightarrow{\bar{\alpha}_p} \mathbb{1}$$

$$\frac{\rho \xrightarrow{\alpha_{x;q}} \rho'}{<\rho> .p \xrightarrow{\alpha_q} <\rho'> .p[x := q]}$$

$$\frac{\rho \dot{=} \varepsilon \quad p \xrightarrow{a} p'}{<\rho> .p \xrightarrow{a} p'}$$

$$(\gamma) \quad \frac{p \xrightarrow{a} p' \quad q \xrightarrow{b} q' \quad a \frown b}{(p \odot q) \xrightarrow{\tau} (p' \odot q')}$$

$$\frac{p \xrightarrow{\tau} p'}{\bar{\alpha}p \xrightarrow{\tau} \bar{\alpha}p'}$$

$$\frac{p \xrightarrow{\tau} p'}{<\rho> .p \xrightarrow{\tau} <\rho> p'}$$

$$\frac{p \xrightarrow{\tau} p'}{(p \odot q) \xrightarrow{\tau} (p' \odot q)}$$

$$\frac{q \xrightarrow{\tau} q'}{(p \odot q) \xrightarrow{\tau} (p \odot q')}$$

$$\frac{p \xrightarrow{a} p'}{(p \mid q) \xrightarrow{a} (p' \mid q)}$$

$$\frac{q \xrightarrow{b} q'}{(p \mid q) \xrightarrow{b} (p \mid q')}$$

$$\frac{p \xrightarrow{a} p' \quad q\dagger}{(p \odot q) \xrightarrow{a} p'}$$

$$\frac{q \xrightarrow{b} q' \quad p\dagger}{(p \odot q) \xrightarrow{b} q'}$$

The rule labelled (γ) is at the heart of the γ-calculus. If p and q are capable of complementary actions producing p' and q', then the cooperation of p and q may perform a silent action to become the cooperation of p' and q'. This rule describes how terms, as processes, may communicate with one another. The last two rules state that a cooperation may only have "external" relations (i.e. sending and receiving) if one of the components has become idle; otherwise the only actions that a cooperation can perform are silent.

Relationships between terms (and actions) are established via bisimulations. If $R \subseteq \Gamma \times \Gamma$ is a relation on terms then we extend it to a relation on actions, $\hat{R} \subseteq \mathcal{A} \times \mathcal{A}$, in the following way:

$$a\hat{R}b \Leftrightarrow a = b \vee \exists \alpha \in N \; \exists p, q.pRq \; \& \; a = \bar{\alpha}_p \; \& \; b = \bar{\alpha}_q$$

Definition 9.15 $R \subseteq \Gamma \times \Gamma$ *is:*

(i) a strong simulation if it satisfies:

> **S1**: $pRq \; \& \; p\sigma \xrightarrow{a} p' \Rightarrow \exists b.a\hat{R}b \; \exists q'.p'Rq' \; \& \; q\sigma \xrightarrow{b} q'$
>
> **S2**: $pRq \; \& \; p\dagger \Rightarrow q\dagger$

(ii) a strong bisimulation if it is a symmetric strong simulation.

Proposition 9.16 *The congruence $\equiv$ is a strong simulation on Γ.*

Exercise 9.2.2 *Provide a proof of the above proposition. You will need to use the fact that:*

> *If R is a strong simulation then $pRq \Rightarrow p\sigma Rq\sigma$ for all substitutions σ*

and proceed by induction on the proof that $p\sigma \equiv q\sigma$ and then induction on the proof of the transition $p\sigma \xrightarrow{a} p'$.

This allows us to define the transition relation $\rightarrow$ on $\Gamma/ \equiv$. Consequently, by an abuse of notation, we can write:

$$(\alpha x.p \odot \bar{\alpha}q) \rightarrow p[x := q]$$

which should be beginning to look familiar (compare it with the rule (β) from the λ-calculus).

9.2.2   Relating the γ-calculus to the λ-calculus

The γ-calculus is an extension of the λ-calculus. To demonstrate this we define a mapping from λ-terms to γ-terms:

Definition 9.17 *We define the mapping $\Theta : \Lambda \rightarrow \Gamma$ as follows:*

$$\Theta x = x$$
$$\Theta(\lambda x.M) = < \lambda x > .\Theta M$$
$$\Theta(MN) = (\Theta M \odot \bar{\lambda}(\Theta N))$$

We assume that substitution in the two calculi are defined in the same way and thus:

$$\forall M, N \in \Lambda.\Theta(M[x := N]) = (\Theta M)[x := \Theta N]$$

The central result relating the two calculi is:

Proposition 9.18 *For all $M, N \in \Lambda$:*
  (i) $M \rightarrow_\beta N \Rightarrow \exists P \equiv \Theta N$ *such that* $\Theta M \rightarrow P$
  (ii) $\Theta M \rightarrow P \Rightarrow \exists N \in \Lambda.M \rightarrow_\beta N$ & $\Theta N \equiv P$

Proof
(i) induction over the definition of $\rightarrow_\beta$.
(ii) structural induction on M.   □

Part (i) of the above proposition states that for each one-step reduction on λ-terms, there is a corresponding transition on the γ-terms. Part (ii) states that starting from the translation of a λ-term, each γ-transition is matched by a corresponding reduction.

Exercise 9.2.3 *Complete the proof of the above proposition.*

The proposition establishes an equivalence between the λ-calculus and a sub-calculus of the γ-calculus. If Θ was surjective then the two calculi would be equally powerful; however there are γ-terms which cannot be considered as the translation of any λ-term. To see this consider the coding of disjunction in the two calculi. In Chapter 6, we introduced an encoding for the truth values and invited the reader to encode various logical operations; a suitable encoding for or would be:

$$\lambda xy.(x\mathbf{T})y$$

the corresponding γ-term is:

$$< \lambda x.\lambda y > .(x\mathbf{T})y$$

(for suitable encoding of $\mathbf{T}$ in the γ-calculus). Notice that both of these operators are "sequential": no answer is produced until the first argument has been evaluated to normal form — there is a preferred ordering on the evaluation of arguments. A fundamental theorem of the λ-calculus, due to Berry, is that all λ-terms denote sequential functions. Herein lies the major difference between the two calculi; an alternative representation of disjunction in the γ-calculus is:

$$< \lambda x \mid \lambda y > .(x\mathbf{T})y$$

which is sometimes called *parallel or.* This alternative disjunction exploits non-determinism to evaluate to $\mathbf{T}$ if either of the arguments does, even if the other term is not normalising.

9.3   The $\lambda\sigma$-calculus

We now return to a calculus which is intended to be equivalent to the λ-calculus. In the classical λ-calculus, which has been our main subject in this book, substitution is an extra-logical feature. In contrast, in the $\lambda\sigma$-calculus the operation of substitution is "built-in" to the calculus in the form of *closure* terms. There are various versions of the λσ-calculus: a type-free calculus, a first-order calculus (corresponding to the simple typed λ-calculus) and a second-order calculus (with polymorphic types). We will concentrate (exclusively) on the type-free calculus; in this setting the explicit handling of substitution is suggestive of abstract machine structures to support the calculus as we have already seen for the λρ-calculus in Chapter 8.

9.3.1 The basic theory of the λσ-calculus

Terms in the λσ-calculus are either λ-terms in de Bruijn notation with indices starting from 1 (see Chapter 2) or closure terms. Consequently the substitutions apply to de Bruijn indexes. Terms and substitutions are constructed from the alphabet:

1	the de Bruijn index
λ	
[,]	closure brackets
id	the identity substitution
↑	shift
·	cons
∘	composition

Definition 9.19 *We define $\mathcal{A}$, the class of terms and $\mathcal{S}$, the class of substitutions, to be the least classes defined by:*
(i) $1 \in \mathcal{A}$ *and* $id, ↑ \in \mathcal{S}$.
(ii) If $a, b \in \mathcal{A}$ *and* $s, t \in \mathcal{S}$:

$$ab, \ \lambda a, \ a[s] \in \mathcal{A}$$

$$a \cdot s, \ s \circ t \in \mathcal{S}$$

A substitution is a mapping $Num \to \mathcal{A}$. We will often write the elements of a substitution explicitly in braces ({ and }). id is the identity substitution $\{i := i\}$; ↑ is a shift substitution $\{i := i+1\}$; $a \cdot s$ prefixes the term a onto s giving the substitution $\{1 := a, i+1 := s(i)\}$; $s \circ t$ is the composition of two substitutions $\{i := s(i)[t]\}$.

Given our discussion of substitutions it should be clear why the syntax of terms only includes the index 1; any other index ($n+1$, say) can be encoded by:

$$1[↑^n]$$

where the superscript n represents an iterated sequence of ↑s.

The theory λσ is generated from the following axioms, which define a notion of reduction (in the sense of Chapter 3). The first axiom is called Beta and the remaining ten axioms are called σ:

$$(\lambda a)b \qquad = a[b \cdot id]$$

$$
\begin{aligned}
1[id] &= 1 \\
1[a \cdot s] &= a \\
(ab)[s] &= (a[s])(b[s]) \\
(\lambda a)[s] &= \lambda(a[1 \cdot (s \circ \uparrow)]) \\
a[s][t] &= a[s \circ t]
\end{aligned}
$$

$$
\begin{aligned}
id \circ s &= s \\
\uparrow \circ id &= \uparrow \\
\uparrow \circ (a \cdot s) &= s \\
(a \cdot s) \circ t &= a[t] \cdot (s \circ t) \\
(s \circ s') \circ s'' &= s \circ (s' \circ s'')
\end{aligned}
$$

The second group of axioms concern the distribution of substitutions through terms, the final group concerns the simplification of substitutions.

The theory $\lambda\sigma$ can be generated from the notion of reduction in the "usual" way. We will not pursue this here; later we will develop a one-step reduction relation which represents leftmost reduction to weak head normal form. For now we turn to the relationship with the λ-calculus.

9.3.2   Relating the $\lambda\sigma$-calculus to the λ-calculus

The normal notion of β-reduction is not included directly in the $\lambda\sigma$-calculus: the rule Beta does not equate to β because the right-hand side of Beta is a closure term involving an explicit substitution whereas the β-rule does the substitution. The definition of β-reduction in the de Bruijn notation is:

$$(\lambda a)b \to_\beta a\{b/1, 1/2, \ldots, n/n+1, \ldots\}$$

where the meta-level substitution operation $\{\ldots\}$ is defined by the following proof system:

$$n\{a_1/1, \ldots, a_n/n, \ldots\} = a_n$$

$$\frac{a\{a_1/1, \ldots, a_n/n, \ldots\} = a' \quad b\{a_1/1, \ldots, a_n/n, \ldots\} = b'}{(ab)\{a_1/1, \ldots, a_n/n, \ldots\} = a'b'}$$

$$\frac{a_i\{2/1, \ldots, n+1/n, \ldots\} = a_i' \quad a\{1/1, a_1'/2, \ldots, a_n'/n+1, \ldots\} = a'}{(\lambda a)\{a_1/1, \ldots, a_n/n, \ldots\} = \lambda a'}$$

The effect of this operation is to perform the substitution and renaming required by the definition of substitution in the de Bruijn calculus (see Chapter 2).

The following proposition relates this meta-level substitution operation to the explicit substitutions:

Proposition 9.20 *If there exist m and p such that $a_{m+q} = p + q$ for all $q \geq 1$, and $a\{a_1/1, \ldots, a_n/n, \ldots\} = b$ is provable in the formal system above, then the σ-normal form of $a[a_1 \cdot a_2 \cdot \ldots \cdot a_m \cdot \uparrow^p] = b$.*

Proof
By induction on the length of the proof of $a\{a_1/1, \ldots, a_n/n, \ldots\} = b$.   □

The importance of the above proposition is that it establishes that we can simulate β-reduction by first performing a Beta step followed by a series of σ-reductions to σ-normal form.

Exercise 9.3.1 *Prove the above proposition. You may find it helpful to strengthen the result to argue that all intermediate terms in the derivation satisfy the hypothesis.*

We state (without proof — or exercises!) the following results:

- Beta+σ is CR
- σ is SN and CR
- β is CR on σ-normal forms

The last two results, and some of our preceding discussion, require the notion of σ-normal form. So far we have relied on intuition as to the form that such terms should take. We close this subsection by formalising this notion. A substitution in normal form is necessarily of the form:

$$a_1 \cdot (a_2 \cdot (\ldots (a_m \cdot U) \ldots))$$

where U is either id or a shift, $\uparrow^n$. A term in normal form is entirely free from substitutions except in subterms of the form $1[\uparrow^n]$ which encode the de Bruijn indexes.

9.3.3   Towards an abstract machine

In this section we present two variants of a one-step, leftmost outermost reduction strategy. Both are suggestive of abstract machine studies. The reader should refer back to Chapter 8 for a related discussion of abstract machines.

Both of the strategies are weak reduction strategies (compare with combinatory logic): they both reduce to whnf.

Definition 9.21 *A weak head normal form is a $\lambda\sigma$ term of the form:*
(i) λa
or
(ii) $na_1 \ldots a_m$

We start by defining a relation $\overset{n}{\rightarrow}$. Recall that in Chapter 3, we generated the one-step reduction relation from the corresponding notion by taking the compatible closure. Since we are interested in leftmost reduction only and are only evaluating to whnf (i.e. not evaluating under λs), we just add:

$$\frac{a \overset{n}{\rightarrow} a'}{ab \overset{n}{\rightarrow} a'b}$$

We also add two rules for substitutions:

$$\frac{s \overset{n}{\rightarrow} s'}{1[s] \overset{n}{\rightarrow} 1[s']}$$

$$\frac{s \overset{n}{\rightarrow} s'}{\uparrow \circ\, s \overset{n}{\rightarrow} \uparrow \circ\, s'}$$

and orientate the eleven axioms left-to-right (replacing $=$ by $\overset{n}{\rightarrow}$).

The following proposition relates $\overset{n}{\rightarrow}$ to leftmost outermost one-step β-reduction.

Proposition 9.22 *If* $a \overset{n}{\rightarrow} b$ *then, given* a' *and* b' *the* σ-*nfs of* a *and* b, *either* $a' \overset{n}{\rightarrow}_\beta b'$ *or* a' *and* b' *are identical. The* $\overset{n}{\rightarrow}$ *reduction of* a *terminates iff the leftmost outermost* β-*reduction of* a' *terminates.*

The second approach, $\overset{wn}{\rightarrow}$, involves an optimisation of $\overset{n}{\rightarrow}$: the rule

$$((\lambda a)[s])b \overset{wn}{\rightarrow} a[b \cdot s]$$

replaces the two rules:

$$(\lambda a)b \;\overset{n}{\rightarrow} a[b \cdot id]$$
$$(\lambda a)[s] \overset{n}{\rightarrow} \lambda(a[1 \cdot (s \circ \uparrow)])$$

This optimisation is justified by the following:

$$
\begin{aligned}
((\lambda a)[s])b &\rightarrow \lambda(a[1 \cdot (s \circ \uparrow)])b \\
&\rightarrow a[1 \cdot (s \circ \uparrow)][b \cdot id] \\
&\rightarrow a[(1 \cdot (s \circ \uparrow)) \circ (b \cdot id)] \\
&\rightarrow a[1[b \cdot id] \cdot ((s \circ \uparrow) \circ (b \cdot id))] \\
&\rightarrow a[b \cdot (s \circ \uparrow) \circ (b \cdot id)] \\
&\rightarrow a[b \cdot (s \circ (\uparrow \circ (b \cdot id)))] \\
&\rightarrow a[b \cdot (s \circ id)] \\
&= a[b \cdot s]
\end{aligned}
$$

The last step above uses the (reasonable) rule:

$$s \circ id = s$$

This rule is not part of $\overset{n}{\to}$; thus the two strategies are different. Both are weak strategies in the sense that they do not evaluate under abstractions but the second strategy doesn't even pass substitutions into abstractions. This last observation suggests that $\overset{wn}{\to}$ models environment machines, whereas $\overset{n}{\to}$ is more closely related to combinator reduction machines.

9.4 Summary

We have presented three new calculi: the lazy λ-calculus, the γ-calculus and the $\lambda\sigma$-calculus. Each extends the classical λ-calculus in some way. We have seen two new techniques:

- the use of *bisimulations* to establish relationships between terms (as opposed to convertibility).
- a refined notion of compatible closure (see Chapter 3) which allows us to enforce particular reduction strategies.

The notion of bisimulation was first introduced in the context of process-based languages. The view taken is that a term is a *black box*; properties of the term can be determined by performing *experiments* on the box. If two boxes behave in the same way in response to every possible experiment then they are indistinguishable (with respect to the given bisimulation). In the lazy λ-calculus an experiment takes the form of an application of the "box" to some term; the response to an experiment is an indication of convergence or divergence — this is the only property of a term that is "observable". In the γ-calculus, experiments are also applications and convergence also plays a part in the response, but experiments also include some information about the ports that are used.

10

Further Reading

10.1 General

We have given a Computer Science perspective on the material covered in this book. Many of the fundamental results have been produced by logicians. Our inspiration in writing this book has been Barendregt's encyclopaedic tome [5]. Most of the basic material presented here is treated in much more detail in [5] and the interested reader is urged to consult it. The classical presentation of the λ-calculi is Church's 1941 report [10].

One of the earliest textbooks in the field was Hindley, Lercher and Seldin's *Introduction to Combinatory Logic*; while this is no longer available, [17] is a much-expanded treatment of the same material. The latter is written from a mathematical logician's perspective, so it is short on computational intuitions, but it is nonetheless a useful reference, particularly for material on typed calculi.

A number of functional programming textbooks contain computing-oriented descriptions of the λ-calculus and combinators. For example [16, 21, 22] contain accounts of the main results relating to functional languages and their implementation.

[23] is a detailed bibliography of work published up until 1982.

The de Bruijn notation, introduced in Chapter 2, is studied in detail in [11].

10.2 Reduction

A more detailed consideration of evaluation strategies for functional languages and the relevance of the λ-calculus to such languages may be found in [16]. The basic material of this chapter is drawn from [5]. The material on labelled reduction and residuals is based on the approach used by Klop in [20].

10.3 Combinatory Logic

Combinatory logic is the main focus of [17]. Historically, the main references to this work are [13, 14] but these are not for the fainthearted!

10.4   Semantics

A comprehensive treatment of semantics may be found in [5] and [17]. Both include detailed discussions of Scott's models. Barendregt's book also includes extensive material on Böhm trees. Stoy's book [24] is the classical textbook on denotational semantics and contains a good introduction to the λ-calculus and models. There have been a number of books published recently which contain some coverage of this material; a good example is [25].

10.5   Computability

Computability aspects of the Lambda Calculus and Combinatory Logic are dealt with in [5] and [17]. A more general treatment of this subject (which does not even mention the various calculi considered here!) may be found, for example, in [18].

10.6   Types

In [5] the main focus is on type-free calculi; there is a short appendix on the simple typed λ-calculus. For a more detailed and up-to-date treatment of typed calculi, [7] is recommended. A large part of [17] is devoted to typed calculi and [19] contains a number of seminal papers on the polymorphic λ-calculus.

10.7   Practical Issues

Abstract machines are considered in [11, 12, 16, 21, 22]; our material is mainly based on [12]. The analysis to detect needed reductions is introduced in [6]. Abstract interpretation is an extremely active area of research at present; the collection [2] contains some tutorial material and a detailed bibliography. [9] emphasises the use of abstract interpretation in the analysis and compilation of typed functional programming languages. The material on Milner's algorithm is based on [15].

10.8   Other Calculi

The lazy lambda calculus was introduced by Abramsky in [3]; our proof of the equivalence of the bisimulation and contextual congruences is based on [4].

The γ-calculus is described in [8] and the λσ-calculus is reported in [1].

10.9   Summary

In constructing this "bibliography" we have restricted our attention to material that is readily accessible; except in a few cases, this has meant that we have cited books. Many of the most fundamental and exciting results have appeared and continue to appear in conference proceedings and journals. Good starting points are the ACM *Principles of Programming Languages*, the proceedings of a conference which is held annually, and the proceedings of the *European Symposium on Programming* (ESOP), which is held every two years.

Bibliography

[1] M. Abadi, L. Cardelli, P.-L. Curien and J.-J. Lévy, Explicit Substitutions, in *Proceedings of POPL'90*, ACM Press, 1990.

[2] S. Abramsky and C. L. Hankin, *Abstract Interpretation of Declarative Languages*, Ellis Horwood, 1987.

[3] S. Abramsky, The Lazy Lambda Calculus, in *Research Topics in Functional Programming*, D. Turner (ed), Addison Wesley, 1990.

[4] S. Abramsky and C.-H. L. Ong, Full Abstraction in the Lazy Lambda Calculus, Technical Report, University of Cambridge, 1991. To appear in *Information and Computation*.

[5] H. P. Barendregt, *The Lambda Calculus: Its Syntax and Semantics*, 2nd edition, North Holland, 1984.

[6] H. P. Barendregt, J. R. Kennaway, J. W. Klop and M. R. Sleep, Needed Reduction and Spine Strategies for the Lambda Calculus, *Information and Computation* 75(3), December 1987.

[7] H. P. Barendregt, Lambda Calculi with Types, in *Handbook of Logic in Computer Science, Volume II*, S. Abramsky, D. Gabbay and T. S. E. Maibaum (eds), Oxford University Press, 1992.

[8] G. Boudol, Towards a Lambda-Calculus for Concurrent and Communicating Systems, in *Proceedings of CAAP'89*, Springer Verlag LNCS 351, 1989.

[9] G. L. Burn, *Abstract Interpretation and the Parallel Evaluation of Functional Languages*, Pitman, 1991.

[10] A. Church, *The Calculi of Lambda Conversion*, Princeton University Press, 1941.

[11] P.-L. Curien, *Categorical Combinators, Sequential Algorithms and Functional Programming*, 2nd edition, Birkhäuser, 1993.

[12] P.-L. Curien, *An Abstract Framework for Environment Machines*, LIENS-CNRS Report, July 1990.

[13] H. B. Curry, R. Feys and W. Craig, *Combinatory Logic, Volume I*, North Holland, 1958.

[14] H. B. Curry, J. R. Hindley and J. P. Seldin, *Combinatory Logic, Volume II*, North Holland, 1972.

[15] L. Damas and R. Milner, Principal Type Schemes for Functional Programs, in *Proceedings of POPL'82*, ACM Press,

1982.

[16] A. J. Field and P. G. Harrison, *Functional Programming*, Addison Wesley, 1988.

[17] J. R. Hindley and J. P. Seldin, *Introduction to Combinators and λ-Calculus*, Cambridge University Press, 1986.

[18] J. E. Hopcroft and J. D. Ullman, *Introduction to Automata Theory, Languages and Computation*, Addison Wesley, 1979.

[19] G. Huet, *Logical Foundations of Functional Programming*, Addison Wesley, 1990.

[20] J. W. Klop, *Combinatory Reduction Systems*, CWI Report, Amsterdam, 1980.

[21] S. L. Peyton Jones, *The Implementation of Functional Programming Languages*, Prentice Hall International, 1987.

[22] C. Reade, *Elements of Functional Programming*, Addison Wesley, 1989.

[23] A. Rezus, *A Bibliography of Lambda-Calculi, Combinatory Logics and Related Topics*, CWI Report, Amsterdam, 1982.

[24] J. E. Stoy, *Denotational semantics: the Scott–Strachey approach to programming language theory*, MIT Press, 1977.

[25] G. Winskel, *The Formal Semantics of Programming Languages*, MIT Press, 1993.

Index